KT-467-696

A LIFETIME OF NOTES
The Memoirs of Tomás Ó Canainn

BISHOPSTOWN
LIBRARY

The Collins Press

To Bridie Murphy from Carnanban and
Hugh Canning from Kilhoyle in the
County Derry

CORK CITY
9471821
LIBRARIES

Acknowledgements

Audio-Visual Services, University College Cork for the front cover
photograph
Comhaltas Ceoltóirí Eireann for back cover photograph

Back cover photographs feature Tomás Ó Canainn and Derry dancer
Frank Roddy on Comhaltas American tour, and
Na Filí, featuring, from the left, Matt Cranitch, Tom Barry
and Tomás Ó Canainn

Published by The Collins Press, Carey's Lane, The Huguenot
Quarter, Cork 1996

© Tomás Ó Canainn

All rights reserved.
No part of this publication may
be reproduced or transmitted
in any form or by any means,
electronic, mechanical, photocopying,
recording or otherwise without
written permission of the publishers,
or else under the terms of any licence
permitting limited copying issued by
The Irish Copyright Licensing Agency,
The Writer's Centre, 19 Parnell Square, Dublin 1.
British Library cataloguing in publication data.

Printed in Ireland by Colour Books Ltd., Dublin.

Jacket Design by Upper Case Ltd, Cornmarket Street, Cork.

ISBN: 1-898256-18-7

CONTENTS

THE FAMILY IN DERRY

Derry was a fine place in my youth – a city for a young fellow to remember forever, as I have and will. It wasn't rich, of course, but it had a great heart. I was brought up in Pennyburn, on the outskirts of the city, in a mixed community, but I don't remember any bitterness about religion. That was a subject both sides avoided in conversation, but an awareness of religion was a standard part of everyone's make-up in those days. What I do remember is the strong feeling of Irishness that we Catholics had. For me, it was a dream that was bound up with the sectarian divide – the feeling that there was something outside the Northern system – a place or a set of circumstances in which I could find a personal satisfaction, a feeling of self-worth in a bigger community.

These are the words I put on it all now, but I would have expressed it differently then, not knowing what would be possible, even conceivable, in the future. I put the feeling I am talking about in the same mental box that contains an unexpressed desire for something wonderful, a marvellous happening that is waiting for me somewhere out there. The unfulfilled desire to experience it is there for as long as I can remember. Since I cannot easily climb into other people's minds, I don't know if this is a common experience or not: I only know that it is an ever-present with me, something like background printing in a computer, which can continue without unduly interfering with the main function of the machine.

Perhaps it has something to do with losing my father when I was young; perhaps not. My father was Hugh Canning from Kilhoyle, near Drumsurn in County Derry and he married my mother, Bridie Murphy, from Carnanban, three miles out, on the other side of Dungiven. Kilhoyle, set on the slope of the mountain, is clearly visible from Carnanban, though it is some eight miles away. I often think of my mother, when she was young, looking across the flat lands of Dungiven to the distant mountain home of her sweetheart.

Both families were farmers, though Kilhoyle was more involved with sheep-farming on the mountain, while Carnanban tilled the soil and kept cattle. The family traditions say that my mother's people came from the south a very long time ago, but my brother, who is deeply into genealogy, doubts this. I think it may have been just a nationalist family's desire to claim relationship with the Murphys of Wexford. There is definite evidence, however, that my father's people came originally from Inishowen in County Donegal.

My mother's father was Francey Murphy: he was the local fiddler and could sing as well. Another Murphy relation lived at the top of the hill, which was called Strone: he was John Murphy, but was always known as Strone John. By all accounts they were two happy men, who often had musical sessions in my mother's home in Carnanban. Strone John was an excellent singer and a most welcome guest.

I never met either of these men, but I feel I know them well, through the stories of my mother, who was an admirer of both of them. I think it interesting that even though my mother and all her sisters could play the fiddle to a greater or lesser extent, it was only her lone brother, my Uncle Patrick, who was locally recognised as a fiddler. It was not considered proper at the time for a woman to practise such activities. Those were macho times, alright.

Even two lifetimes later, when I used to go on holidays to Carnanban, there was still the same quasi-adoration of 'the men', which is how my Uncle Patrick and my cousins, coming in from their work in the fields, were referred to. My female cousins and my Aunt would all disappear into the back kitchen, to give pride of place to 'the men', a title which included me, when I'd go toiling in the fields with them from about the age of fourteen, working with corn, hay or lint. After the evening meal, Uncle Patrick would sometimes take the fiddle down from its hook at the fireplace to play a few tunes, while some of my cousins would play the

8

mouth-organ. Aunt Kate would give the signal when it was time to say the Rosary and we'd all kneel down, elbows on chair-seats and mumble the responses, as we played a continuous game of nipping or kicking each other, unknown to my Aunt, Uncle and older cousins.

Francey Murphy, as I understand it from my mother's stories, was a good man, but I am sure he was at times what my grandmother would regard as a sore test of her patience, when he'd prefer to play his fiddle rather than be out in the fields working. I had a dream about him one night some years ago and it was the starting point for a poem which I wrote about him. In a way, the dream was as much about my Uncle Patrick and his sisters: I called the poem *To my Grandfather, Francey Murphy*. Someone suggested I should send it to *The Irish Times*, who published it soon afterwards, leading me to believe that being a poet was easy, with *The Irish Times* just waiting to receive my most recent efforts. *Ní mar síltear bítear*! Anyway, here it is:

I saw your Patrick in my sleep last night,
Without his fiddle in his hand,
Gaunt and stumbling towards an open grave,
Where in bright gold they cut his name
Just below yours, Francey, on the weathered stone,
With plenty of room below for the others,
All travelling towards me on moving ground –
Kate and Maggie and Rose going into earth.

But I neither stopped nor turned, but walked
Away against the moving ground
And gained again the place where I'd listen
For the tiny sound that is you in me,
Pulsing now these twenty years
Since first I knew the shouted whisper,
And you even then a lifetime in earth;
Calling long with all the voices
That told their lives and none to listen –
No-one in tune, no more than I,
Who gathered all the early stories
In the mother-talk of your daughter to me.

It was your note she struck and your laugh,
The bell of your voice and your song's dream,
When you should have been like the other men,
Out sneddin' turnips on a windy hill.

9

When your rosined bow livened a reel on the strings
My mother's own mother cried for you
To leave that damned fiddle and put your scythe
To the waiting corn in McFarland's field.

My mother used to tell us about Strone John coming down the
hill from Strone on his ceilí, as they used to call it – in
other words, an evening visit. She'd talk about his habit of
holding his cap up to the side of his head as he'd sing his
songs. His best-known song was *The Verdant Braes of
Screen*, one that I have been singing for years now in his
memory.

My mother, in company with everyone in Carnanban,
was shocked by what happened when poor Strone John
died. He had always attended mass in Dungiven church,
even though he was officially in the parish of Banagher, a
long distance away. The priest in Dungiven refused to let
Strone John be buried in the hallowed ground of Dungiven
cemetery, since he didn't belong to the parish and paid his
dues in Banagher. The result was that he was buried beside
the ditch, outside what was regarded as consecrated
ground. I am glad to say that many years later, when the
graveyard was expanded, John's grave came to have an
important place in the new arrangement.

I tried to get something of my negative feelings about
the affair out of my system in a poem I wrote some years ago
called *The Ballad of Strone John*. It uses some lines from
John's song, *The Verdant Braes of Screen*, with slight
changes in the final verse, to suit the story I have to tell:

He crossed the burn in a crooked line
Jumping to each dry stone
An old man abroad on his ceilí
Bringing a song from Strone.

Oh, sit ye down on the grass, he said,
*On the dewy grass so green,
For the wee birds all have come and gone
Since you my love have been*, he said,
Since you my love have been.

The song in his mouth was like the man
– Wrack from another tide,

10

With syllables floating on every note
As he feathered his mountainy rhyme
Over *The Verdant Braes of Screen*
Where the wee birds all had flown
And love was filled with the thousand notes
He carried down from Strone.

The singer is gone but his song rings
To spite the man of God
Who refused him a place to lie with his friends
Beneath the well-kept sod;
So he was laid in unhallowed ground
By the priest who had no ear,
Like a dog by a ditch at Dungiven church
For paying his dues elsewhere.

Oh let me lie beneath the grass,
Beneath the grass so green,
For the wee birds all have come and gone
Since you and I have been, he said,
Since you and I have been.

By the time my parents married, my father was an engineer
on a cargo boat which operated out of Glasgow. My mother
lived in Glasgow, of course, but would come back to Ireland,
to her sister Kathleen in Derry, for the birth of her babies.
Thus it was that I was born in Derry, the second child, after
my sister Bridie, but spent the first six months of my life in
Glasgow.

When my father took a job on a boat working out of
Coleraine, we came to live there. When I was four, my
father was taken ill at sea and the captain wanted to put
him ashore at Belfast, so that he could get treatment, but
my father insisted that he wanted to get back to Coleraine,
where his family were. At this time there were four children in our family, Josie and Hugh having followed Bridie
and myself into the world! My mother was three months
pregnant at the time.

The captain gave my father whiskey to ease his pain,
but what they didn't know was that he had appendicitis
and whiskey was not the right option in the circumstances.
There was evidently a long delay at Portrush when they
blew the horn to get a lifeboat out to bring him ashore. The
upshot of it all was that he died within the week in

hospital with a burst appendix. It must have been a heart-rending time for my mother, as family tradition has it that he spent a lot of time in a delirious condition, singing his favourite songs, for he was a fine singer. Two of the songs were *The Road to the Isles* and *The Old Bog Road*.

Soon after the funeral, the family moved to Derry, to a house in Barry Street, so that we would be near my Aunt and Uncle in Meadowbank Avenue. The miracle is that my mother somehow managed to rear the five of us (Margaret was born six months after my father's death). My Aunt Kathleen and Uncle Mannie in Meadowbank were towers of strength of course, but my mother trod a long hard road, whose end she reached only a few years ago, at the age of 92. She always told us that pride was a sin, but I hold it no sin to be proud of her. A few years before she died I tried to say something about her in a poem called *Absence*:

> In this pause, before the last Murphy of Carnanban
> Draws down the narrow door, rejoins her five
> Sisters and Patrick (can it be fifteen
> Years since your dying brother, opening his eyes,
> Surprised you with: *Bridie, you may douse*
> *The candles – I'm not away yet?*) I confess
> My fear of imagining your unimaginable
> Absence from a house in Belfast,
> Where you harvested each small success
> Of sons and daughters, (especially of sons!)
> Who have begun to mourn before you're gone.

I don't know if she read that one or not – I was always a bit wary about showing her things like that. I remember giving her a copy of my autobiographical novel based on my early life in my native city, *Home to Derry*, when it was first published and being on tenterhooks until she read it, for it said things about our life in Derry that I was afraid she might not like told. The next time I came to Belfast, where the family lived then, she had finished the book. 'What did you think of it?' I asked her casually. 'Oh, it was good,' she said, 'quite funny.' I waited, for I knew she wasn't finished. 'But you didn't make us any richer than we were,' she said.

Three years after my mother's death, I found myself
dialling her Belfast number, just to have a chat. Soon after
that, during a carol service in Cork, I began to think of all
the obvious things I must have learned from her during my
early life. I wrote about it later and named the poem after
the carol that had started my line of thought – *Silent
Night*. It brought me back to early days in Derry.

SILENT NIGHT

I don't remember
A time I didn't know
That song. Did I learn it
So long ago from you

I don't remember?

I thought of that last night
In St Mary's as I sang
And suddenly the startled words
Stalled in my throat.
'Sleep in ...' was alright
But no word of *'Heavenly peace'*,
Only a kaleidoscope of days

I don't remember.

Derry days and the seventh seat
From the front in Pennyburn Church,
On the left, of course, and the five
Of us marshalled by you,
Making sure we knelt
Up straight, no leaning back:
Was that a venial sin?

I don't remember.

Kaleidoscopic confusion of years,
Confraternities, confessions, stations,
Hours both Forty and Holy,
October Devotions, Retreats:
*'Remember, O most gracious
Virgin Mary that never ...'*

I don't remember.

Sunday walks around the Branch
And home by the Glen and Duncreggan,
Or out the Greenhall and Culmore,

13

Aiming high for Protestant
Respectability. A harp of green
Paper with golden strings,
Pinning wet shamrock
On my new suit;
The miracle of a twelve-sided
Threepenny-bit tight
In my First Communion fist;
Singing for Saint Columba
And a free day on the ninth
Of June: *'Help thy children*
Here in Derry, Thou
The Holy Church's dove.'
Were you ever at the Long Tower Church
When we sang that with the band?

I don't remember.

Saving for a season ticket
For the Féis, where Guildhall gates
Would yield at last and we'd run
For the best seat with a programme
And a packet of Rowntrees fruit clear
Gums, or we'd be the singing
Haymakers in the Christian Brothers'
Action song – what's this we called it?

I don't remember.

You'd always be there for that
On the Thursday night and tell me
It was nice and then together
We'd walk home at midnight
Down the Strand. Why did I
Think we owned it then?

I don't remember.

Such times of talk, like you,
Are no more, yet even now,
Phone in hand I listen
To the long silence
Of your dead, half-dialled number.
I am a searching child
Cast adrift in my sixties. *'Sleep*
In Heavenly peace.' Did I learn it
So long ago from you?

I don't remember.

Nearly all that I know about my father came to me through my mother, who was, I suggest, still in love with him nearly 60 years after he was dead. I have just two personal memories of my father: at this stage I cannot be sure whether I am actually remembering these things, or just the memory of a child's memory:

Did I imagine
His stubbly chin against my cheek
When he jigged me on his knee;
My screams echoing through the kitchen
When he pretended to let me fall;
That sudden roughness of sleeve-cloth in my hand?

Or the other time
I ran beside him down the quay
To rummage the lockers of his bunk
By the rusting bolts of the hull wall?

For years I have polished
Two memories,
Afraid that they might lose
The image of my father.

TO SCHOOL WITH THE 'WEE NUNS'

Singing was always important in our house, as far back as I can remember. My mother sang and everyone in our family had a gift for singing – all of them better at it than I was! I learned a lot from their singing of the songs they had got at school, with the Mercy nuns up in Francis Street, beside the Cathedral. In fact there were two schools there – what we called the 'wee nuns', which was on the lower side of the street and a much bigger building opposite, that we knew as the 'big nuns'. It wasn't that the nuns in one building were bigger than those in the other, but that the school on the lower side catered for infants only, while the other one, which was a girls-only institution, catered for students up to leaving-school-age, which in those days was fourteen.

I went to school at four years of age to the 'wee nuns' and stayed there until first class. Boys had to leave the 'wee nuns' and find another school when their infant training was done, whereas the girls could cross the road into the 'big nuns', as all my sisters did.

One of my teachers in the wee nuns was Sister Laurence, a big kindly person who used to keep drums, whistles and basic musical instruments, suitable for children, on top of a high cupboard: she would bring them down and let us play them as a special favour, when we were good. Mrs McCabe, who, I discovered fairly recently was the mother of Cathal McCabe, Director of Music in RTE, was, like her colleague Miss Durnin, another inspiring teacher. We were lucky students, for whom nothing was left to chance – I remember Sister Laurence bringing unconsecrated hosts from her convent in Pump Street, where they were made, so that we would know exactly what the real thing would feel like on the tongue on our First Communion day in the Cathedral. We were strictly cautioned not to mention it outside the

16

school, in case of misunderstanding or of giving scandal. Look at that now! I have let the cat out of the bag at last, but I hope Sister Laurence, God be good to her, is in a forgiving mood!

Allowing the host to drop from your tongue onto the floor in those pre-Vatican Two days was almost enough to cause an international incident! I am a little ashamed to admit it, but my big memory of First Communion day – or could it have been Confirmation day, I don't remember – was of getting a new shiny twelve-sided threepenny bit as a present. That was big stuff in those days and the coin, still relatively unknown then, had a solid, comforting feel, squeezed into the palm of my hand, pushed deep down into the trouser-pocket of my new velvet suit.

At the age of twelve I left to go to the Christian Brothers' School on the Lecky Road, which was known as 'The Brow of the Hill', and had a reputation for good teaching and firm discipline. Going to the Christian Brothers involved a big decision, as all my male cousins had gone to Rosemount School, which was nearer, but my mother thought I would do better in the CBS environment. To get to the Brow of the Hill, I had to take a halfpenny ride on the Strand Road bus as far as Great James' Street and walk for something less than a mile along Rossville Street and Lecky Road. It was new territory for someone who had never ventured much beyond Barry Street, Meadowbank and Richmond Crescent. I got on well at the 'Brow', as we called it, and was lucky to have Barney Doherty as my first teacher there. Barney, a popular teacher and a Derryman whom everyone liked, wore plus-fours, which, in case some of my readers may not know, were the baggy trousers, tucked into socks, that golfers still sometimes wear. I remember my mother giving me a new tie to present to him when he was getting married. I still remember the first poem he taught us. It was no gem, but was typical of his approach, which was about enjoyment in education. Stand back – here is the long-remembered masterpiece:

Loofah the bull had two-and-six
To spend all on his own:
He did not care for toffee-stick,
Nor yet for buttered scone;
And so he bought a fishing net
To keep his tail from getting wet!

I did well in the competitive atmosphere of the CBS, where we had Christmas and Summer examinations, from which I garnered some welcome prizes from individual teachers. I claim now that I have always had an interest in learning for its own sake, but maybe prizes, like the pocket-watch I got from Brother McFarland in third class, were the real motivators!

In many ways, that school was a major part of my musical apprenticeship. Three teachers, in particular, were responsible for that – Br Pearse McFarland, newly arrived from Belfast and full of enthusiasm for education and music; Paddy Carlin, a Derry musician who could play piano, sing and conduct a choir; and Tommy Carr, who taught us a lot of songs in class. These three teachers bonded together to prepare us for numerous musical competitions at the annual Derry Féis, which took place in the Derry Guildhall in Easter week. Choirs and solos were their strong point and they saw winning at the Féis as a justification of their teaching, which I am sure it was. We would come back after school and at weekends to practise: our commitment was matched by theirs and everyone was aware that to be picked for a CBS choir was a victory in itself. Brother McFarland tended to concentrate on the smaller, more select Gregorian chant choirs and I learned a lot about the art from singing with him. I have to say, though, that his method involved a continual pattern of weeding out the less talented singers from an original choir of some 50 voices, with the result that he finished up in Easter week with, perhaps, just 15 or 25 individuals, depending on the rules of the competition. That final choir was glorious, by any standard, but the human dimension of the elimination process left a lot of us temporarily scarred.

I was involved in a number of action-songs then and the Christian Brother who organised them was Br Roe from the Technical School. He had a name among the senior boys in what we called the 'Tech', for being tough, but when he dealt with us in preparation for the action-song competition he was the kindest man imaginable. I need hardly say that being the Christian Brothers' entry, we usually won the competition. That's how it was – the Christian Brothers were winners and knew how to work towards winning. I think I learned that lesson from them.

We'd learn plenty of nationalist songs for our annual excursion into north Donegal on a bus, privately hired from the Lough Swilly Bus Company, which operated out of Derry. True to form, our teachers would have pull-down maps made out, showing the route and giving interesting details of the various places we'd visit. I even remember so-called banana lemonade being produced at the first stop-ping point on the route. Those excursion songs were also in-corporated into a series of public shows we put on in St Columb's Hall, with orchestral accompaniment, if you don't mind. I remember being the mother of a crying baby in a play that was included in one such show. The baby was a large doll that I had to bring to rehearsals, much to my em-barrassment!

Brother McFarland asked one day in class if any of us were altar-boys and Danny Gorman and myself put up our hands. He asked us to tell the remainder of the class some of the Latin responses used in the mass, and almost had a seizure when he heard the kind of gibberish we regularly used when serving in Pennyburn Church. Our teacher for altar serving was Aidan Barrett, who had, in his turn, learned the Latin from an older altar-server, who had picked it up somewhat informally from another. I suspect the tradition might even have gone as far back as my cous-in, Patrick Coyle, who had been an altar-boy in the cathe-dral in the mid-1930s, when Pennyburn was first built. He was one of the first altar-boys in the new church. Father O'Loughlin, priest-in-charge at Pennyburn, was a kind, tol-erant man and didn't seem to mind our pronunciation of

Latin, but Br McFarland was determined to undo the damage!

The important thing for a Pennyburn altar-boy in those days was to keep your surplice clean and regularly laundered. My mother was sometimes scandalised by our antics on the altar, but the priests didn't mind too much, as long as we lit the candles and kept the box of candles at Our Lady's shrine on the side-altar full. By replenishing the candle box, parishioners could continue putting money into the slot at the side altar to purcahse and light up the waxen signs of devotion to their deceased relatives. I remember one such parishioner would come up after Saturday-morning mass every week, to light his candle. Whoever was due to refill the box would be watching for the expected move up the aisle. As soon as it happened, one of us altar-boys would time our arrival at the box to coincide with his. Invariably, he would put his hand in his pocket and produce a silver coin as a present. It was like winning the pools or the sweepstake. Mind you, one could get better money for being altar-boy at a wedding, a job which the more senior amongst us tried to keep for themselves. When I was approaching the magic age of being a senior altar-boy – about thirteen, I think – a new priest, Fr McCauley, replaced Fr O'Loughlin and made a complete clear-out of all us thirteen year old lags, replacing us with younger, well-drilled lads of his own choosing. My dreams of wedding riches were over and I have to say there was general agreement that Fr McCauley's clean young recruits were paragons of virtue and good behaviour. I am sure they never had slipper fights in the sacristy or were guilty of stuffing a colleague's surplice up a sooty chimney! Happy days.

Brother McFarland regularly taught singing in his classes – it wasn't just something he took on for concerts and féiseanna. I remember one such class, when he was putting us through our musical warm-up, before the singing proper began. He'd give a note and we would sing up and down an arpeggio to a syllable nominated by him. He'd raise it up a tone then and we would do the same thing. It was good fun and didn't require too much thought. I was in the very back row for this combined class and started doing slightly jazzy variations on Br McFarland's theme, much to the amusement of my friends. Encouraged by their reaction, I took more and more liberties with the original, not noticing that all of a sudden, they had stopped laughing and were dutifully singing the given arpeggio. Suddenly my world was shattered by the most enormous ear-clout I had ever received. I fell sideways with a terrible ringing in my head and ears. Unknown to me, Br McFarland, who had a keen ear, had left the front of the class and walked quietly right around behind us, to find the culprit. I may say that he was also the Physical Training instructor, a former hurler in his Belfast days and possessed of a mightily strong arm. I presume that he had been carefully sizing up his strike while I was doing my final variations on his theme.

I still think the Christian Brothers' primary school on the Brow of the Hill was the best musical academy in Derry in those days. That is saying something, because singing was a very important part of every school in the Maiden City at the time. In fact singing was part of normal Derry life: it was only when I came to Cork, many years later, that I experienced something comparable to the ethos of Derry in this regard.

I think the Christian Brothers were not too happy when, at twelve, I sat the St Columb's College entrance examination and got a scholarship. They expected their better students to continue their studies in their own Tech, when they left the primary school after sixth class. Part of the reason for my going to St Columb's was that it was more or less regarded as the Diocesan seminary and if one wanted to become a priest in the Derry diocese it was almost obligatory that you attend St Columb's and choose Latin and Greek as your main languages. Latin was compulsory, anyway, as was Irish, for all practical purposes.

For years, when asked what I intended to do when I grew up I would reply that I was going to be a priest. However, for a time when I was younger, it seemed that I might become a telegram-boy with the Post Office. The big thing about it was that Catholics had just as good a chance of getting in as Protestants, since it did not depend on local patronage. Most jobs in the Guildhall, i.e., in local administration, were filled by Protestants. Another big plus for the job as a telegram-boy was that you could eventually aspire to an office-job in the main Derry Post Office. But by the time I got the scholarship to St Columb's, all thoughts of becoming a telegram-boy had vanished and I felt I was on course for the priesthood. The Holy Roman Catholic Church had a miraculous escape when I eventually chose engineering. Surely that in itself is a sign of God's protecting hand looking after his own institution!

Even though I didn't formally study music in St Columb's, at least not in my early years, I was in the choir, conducted by John Maultsaid, that sang at all the high masses and ordinations. Mr Maultsaid also taught us geography. In our later years, I remember him starting an evening class in musical appreciation. He was upstairs in the President's room, playing records of Schubert and Beethoven and explaining things to us over the microphone, while we sat in the Senior Study just below. He was also the regular conductor of the brass and reed band that used to play in the grounds of the Long Tower Church for the feast of St Columba, every 9 June, which had been a free day for us when I attended the 'Brow of the Hill'. I was continually surprised that we had to study on St Columb's feastday in St Columb's College, though we always attended the Long Tower service, wearing the oak-leaf in our lapels and singing the St Columba hymn.

By the time I reached my final year in St Columb's, I knew the Church was not my goal. The only alternative was to go for teaching, which had just begun to offer very healthy scholarships, based on the Senior Certificate Examination. When I say 'healthy', I mean what we then considered a *massive* £150 a year, which could, if one was careful, cover tuition and lodgings in Belfast, while attending St Mary's Training College.

Clearly one knew that universities were possibilities for some people, but only if you had access to private funds. Generally speaking they were only available to some of the richer Catholics, who could send their children down to University College Dublin. The two Derry university scholarships had for years been worth a mere £30 each, which made them useless for us. But then, in 1948, the local education authority leaked the information that the sum might be increased. I was lucky enough to get both a university scholarship and what was known as a 'call' to the Training College. Imagine my surprise when I heard that the value of the local university scholarship had been raised to £150. Life was opening out in front of me, yet it didn't really leave me with a choice – I knew it had to be a university – not the Training College. Even the Christian Brothers and the priests in St Columb's were now coming round to the view that students from Derry would do better in the atmosphere of Queen's University than in what they considered the rather *laissez-faire* atmosphere of a slightly decadent UCD. This may come as a surprise to afficionados of the National University!

I went up to Queen's to register along with Éamonn, a classmate who had got the second scholarship – our very first journey so far from home. Neither of us quite knew what we'd do, but in the event, we both finished up in Engineering, partly because Éamonn's brother was already a practising engineer out in the big world and seemed to be doing alright. But the real reason for my choice was probably that my hobbies at the time included constructing small wireless sets and, quite separately, making bangers from sodium chlorate and sulphur. We used to explode our bangers inside the local air-raid shelter, where they'd make the most satisfying boom you could imagine. There were still air-raid shelters in every street in our district, long after the war had become just a memory for everyone else.

My mother viewed our experiments with some trepidation, I can tell you. Her big fear, when we were young, was that we'd join the Republican movement, though we didn't really know what that meant at the time. She was a strong nationalist herself, but viewed my interest in things Irish in two ways. One side of her was for Irish, but the other –

the motherly side – was against it. 'That oul' Irish,' she'd say, 'it's only for mountainy men.' She had seen the last native speakers of County Derry Irish in the Bennedy hills above Dungiven, and her own parents and their neighbours used to bring in Irish speakers from the Donegal gaeltacht to work on the local farms as what they called 'servant boys' and 'servant girls'.

When I got talking to the Adviser of Studies, T.P. Allen, in the Engineering Faculty in Queen's – a great and a good man – I signed on for Electrical Engineering, which surprised a few people when I got back to Derry after my one day trip up to the big city. I discovered that day from T.P. Allen that he was an active radio amateur, in communication with the rest of the world from his own transmitter. I am sure I filed that information in my brain for use at another time, for I eventually became a licensed radio-amateur myself, many years later.

Although Éamonn and I were school-friends in Derry we didn't share digs in Belfast. My companions there were Willie Gorman, a future pharmacist whose mother and mine had secured digs for us in St Paul's parish near the Royal Victoria Hospital, and Tommy Kerrigan, who was training to be a teacher. Éamonn stayed with us once or twice when he was stuck for accomodation just before he forsook Engineering. To be honest, he was far more interested in backing horses and dogs, though his success rate there wasn't at all good. He should never have taken on Engineering. All his talents – and he was prodigiously talented – lay in literature. His essays at school were the sort that Frank McAuley, our English teacher, tore out and stored in his desk, for the edification of future generations of students.

Tommy and I soon realised that our mothers, unknown to us, had arranged with the landlady, a right dour woman, that we should be home before ten o'clock at night, so you'd find us running up the Falls and almost falling into the hallway of our digs at a minute to ten each night, panting after our exertions. Willie set about changing all that when he arrived. Unlike Tommy and me, he was an old-stager in the game of lodgings.

'What's your hurry?' he asked, as we quickened our step past the Falls Baths at a quarter to ten. 'She'll murder us if we're late,' Tommy said, anxiously. 'No rush,' said Willie, slowing us down. We eventually walked in at five past ten to a frosty welcome. Supper was set in front of us, but no word was spoken. It was quarter past ten on the following two nights and then we stretched it to half past for the rest of the week – all part of Willie's master plan.

We just knew it was game, set and match-point for us the night we heard the clocks strike midnight and us still only halfway up the Grosvenor Road. The poor woman gave up the unequal struggle after that. Her three culchies had become city slickers!

A DOUBLE LIFE

I had always been interested in both science and the humanities. Education in the Derry schools that I attended was broadly based and it was taken for granted that a wide range of interests was normal and healthy. While one did eventually have to make a choice at third level, none of us felt that we were thereby inevitably and irrevocably channelled down a single narrow lane. While I was a student at Queen's studying engineering, it seemed normal to hire out a room in Crymble's music shop with a piano, so that I could improve my keyboard skills. Equally, my interest in amateur radio prompted me to try and join the YMCA in Belfast, as they had an active radio club there. One of my fellow-students, a fairly recently demobbed serviceman, told me about it and recommended that I have a word with the secretary of the YM, with a view to becoming a member. That was when I came up against one of the hard facts of Northern life in those times. Once I had filled-in the necessary form, the secretary brought me into his office, and spent some time explaining to me, in the nicest possible way, that I should join a Catholic organisation. However much I tried to tell him that it was the radio club in the YMCA that interested me, he still kept pointing out the advantages of a Catholic club for someone like me. I got the message eventually and left. When I told my fellow-student what had happened, he was furious. Having recently come back from active service with His Majesty's Forces, he just didn't believe that such an attitude was possible anymore. He could hardly wait to talk to the secretary. When he returned, he was full of apologies and obviously deeply disappointed. There had been no change in the situation: I was still an outsider.

The Workers' Educational Association in Belfast used to hold classes in a variety of subjects in those days and I attended one on musical appreciation, given by the music-critic of the *Belfast Telegraph*. I suppose that might even have had some influence on my later move into the perilous waters of music criticism in Cork! Whatever about that, I still remember our lecturer's sensitive playing of a Clementi sonatina and my own subsequent torturing of that harmless and beautiful piece of music in Crymble's upper room, during my hired half-hour there. When I couldn't afford to hire Crymble's – and that was often enough, as the Derry Corporation were sometimes slow in sending the scholarship money – I used to enjoy myself in my lodgings, learning to play a round-backed mandolin, which I had bought cheaply in Smithfield.

It is with some shame that I remember attending a concert by the Reginald Jacques Orchestra, who had included Belfast on their British tour. I met a number of my Derry school pals there. One of my companions talked quite knowledgeably after the concert about Mozart's *Eine Kleine Nachtmusik*, which the orchestra had just played. It was a measure of our rather closed minds that I and the others could not believe that an ordinary fellow from the same background as ourselves could possibly know so much about a composer like Mozart! He had to be bluffing, showing off, we agreed afterwards. That begrudging reaction is what I am still ashamed of today.

When I went to Manchester some time later on a graduate apprenticeship, however, I did get plenty of opportunity to indulge in both science and the humanities. Sometimes the science was mixed up with wheeling barrowloads of coke for a furnace I had to keep stoking when I did my stint of night-duty in the Metrovick foundry. On the graduate-apprenticeship, I was moved around the various departments – sometimes labouring and sometimes, in my best clothes, working in one of the engineering or research offices. Getting an offer of a graduate-apprenticeship at Metropolitan Vickers in Manchester (Metrovick, for short) was regarded as the first step to being what might be called nowadays a captain of industry. The top jobs in the British electrical industry in those days were filled by university graduates who had done their graduate-apprenticeships at either Metrovick or British Thomson-Houston (BTH), the other big company, based in Rugby. The majority of the generating equipment used by the national power company in England was made in either Manchester or Rugby and this Irishman was doing his small bit for the company, either in alternator or transformer testing, or even at the basic level of the foundry. I still remember one of the executives in the company promising that we should reach the dizzy heights of £1,000 per annum by the time we were 30 years of age. This prospect was very attractive from our vantage point of £6.4s.6d. a week! That we did eventually reach the magic thousand had more to do with inflation than anything else, while the bitter wind of international competition in the 1950s blew Metrovick and BTH away.

I found at one stage of my work in the foundry that if I hurried with the shovelling and emptying, I could get five minutes free every quarter of an hour through the night. I used that time to read a book about the series of operas that were then being staged in Manchester. Next evening I would be queueing-up at the door to see the opera about which I had just been reading. It wasn't a bad musical education. When the opera season ended, my life was a little less hectic, though there were still Ralph Hill's books on the symphony and on the concerto to prepare me for twice-weekly trips to the Free-Trade Hall, to hear the splendid Halle Orchestra under John Barbirolli.

I wasn't the only worker there, either. I remember listening to Beethoven's seventh symphony seated beside a ruddy-faced man who didn't stop eating sandwiches, even in the lovely slow movement. As the last note sounded, he jumped to his feet: 'By gum, that were great', he said enthusiastically, in a strong Lancashire accent when he sat down. We got talking at the interval and I discovered that he was an engine-driver who had just brought his engine in to Central Station, which was only a short distance away from the Free Trade Hall. After the concert we said goodbye, hoping to see each other at the next one. I watched him walk away, his working clothes only half-hidden under his overcoat, and I started my journey to Trafford Park, to clock-in at Metrovick, put on my own overalls and begin the long night's work that would earn me my usual wage on Friday evening, when 20,000 of us workers would pour from one of the biggest companies in England.

I got a new appreciation in the Free Trade Hall of the beautiful music that the clarinet could produce. Perhaps I was influenced by the fact that the leader of the clarinet section was an Irishman, by the name of Ryan. I signed-up for clarinet lessons at the Northern School of Music on Oxford Road and was assigned to one of the Halle Orchestra deputies whose name was Wright. I was soon playing simple musical exercises and eventually even had a go at the slow movement of Mozart's famous clarinet concerto, which was probably the work that had inspired me to take up the instrument in the first place. Metrovick was not all about engineering, either: we had a madrigal group there that met regularly and it even had you know who, singing *April is in my Mistress' Face*, with them. I think I called myself a tenor in those days.

One of my fellow-lodgers, John Herring, played soccer for a team called Sale Presbyterian whose home-ground was just a few miles from our digs. He persuaded me to go out there and I finished up as a half-back, tutored by the team-trainer, Jock, who used to be a Scottish international. We had matches every Saturday in the Altrincham Amateur League. The next season we started a team of our own in Metrovick and were accepted into the Lancashire Amateur League, which was of a slightly higher standard than the Altrincham League. We had a good cup run and reached the semi-final, which was surprising in itself, but promised something that was next to immortality – an appearance at Old Trafford in the final. I wish I could write about that, but I can't, as we lost the critical semi-final match. *Sic transit..!*

I got leave of absence to do vacation work in Ireland at the Cathaleen's Falls hydro station in Ballyshannon while I was still with Metrovick. After my sojourn I had to submit a report to the Metrovick Education Department on my Ballyshannon experience. I waxed a little flowery about

29

the beauty of the place, and the fine atmosphere in Ireland and I was called to the Education Department office, where I expected to get a dressing-down about it. Instead of that, Mr Dawney asked would I mind if they published it in the Metrovick journal, *Rotor*! Did I mind?!! Looking back on it, I realise now that this was my very first publication. I probably thought then that it would be my last.

I got job-offers from both the Electricity Supply Board in Dublin and the Electricity Board for Northern Ireland in that Autumn of 1953. The EBNI was based in Belfast and I decided that was where I wanted to be, probably because our family had moved from Derry to Willowbank Gardens, off the Antrim Road in Belfast. My mother had decided that since the centre of gravity of her clutch had moved, she would follow, bringing everything with her. It was strange to be going home and not going to Derry, which had always been the target either from Belfast or from Manchester. Taking the big sweep of Rosses Bay in the LMS (London Midland and Scottish Railway) train and seeing the first glimpse of Pennyburn Church and then the rest of Derry as we steamed towards the Waterside station was always what homecoming had been about. Landing from a boat at an undistinguished Belfast quay and getting a bus up the Antrim Road was hardly a comparable experience.

THE IRISH THING

I wish I knew what chemistry or psychology makes one person interested in certain things and sends someone else, who seems not unlike the first person, down a completely different road. Is an interest, say, in the Irish language, something that grows on a person because they are in an Irish environment or could it be hereditary? I take the Irish language as an example because I assume my particular mental plate was clean and fairly empty of such influences when I was born, yet here I am today speaking Irish all the time at home, after having raised an Irish-speaking family in a kind of mini-gaeltacht just outside Cork city. What makes it more surprising is that I am a Northerner who didn't have Irish at school from the very earliest years, in the way my southern friends had.

When I make this comment to them they tell me that I was lucky not to be affected by the aversion to the language that so many of them suffered. They make the point strongly that this is not just a rationalising of their bias but a strong alienation, quite often based on their antipathy towards authority figures who supported the language. I was surprised to find in discussion that many of the people and organisations I had always regarded as being positive and liberal represented for them something essentially negative and undesirable. Many in Cork claim that organisations like Gael Linn fitted into this category and someone like Pádraig Tyers, whom they saw as the agent in times past for the imposition of compulsory Irish in UCC first-year courses, provoked the same reaction. Hearing this about Pádraig, whom I knew to be motivated by the highest principles, was a real shock and showed me that I and many supporters of the Irish language just did not understand the depth of alienation that was there. Even a symbol like a *fáinne*, worn in someone's coat-lapel, was enough to generate a bad reaction.

I have always been aware that there was a group among Irish-speaking people who regarded themselves almost as owners of the language: I suppose these were the same people who made what used to be called a 'political football' of Irish. I can't say I was ever in this category and I can definitely say that I never had any wish to belong to it. A common feature of religious and cultural groups is that a small percentage of those who believe most strongly are likely to turn their enthusiasm into an intolerant Fascism. In this regard, it is worth saying that Irish has now come back into the ownership of the people, to a much greater degree than 30 years ago when the language was nominally stronger.

I often look back towards my youth to see if I can spot significant moments that engendered my interest in the language. Neither of my parents were Irish-speakers, though when they were young, there were areas near Dungiven where Irish was still spoken. I think, too, that there was an Irish speaker from Donegal labouring for a while in Carnanban so the Irish language would not have been unknown to my mother's people. My impression is that native speakers from Donegal coming in to work in County Derry were not highly regarded and neither, I think, was their language. It was their badge of poverty and, as such, was not something their new neighbours set great store by. There was a lady who lived near the top of our street who had come from Clonmany in Donegal and it was said that she could speak Irish but I have no evidence of that. A cousin of mine in Belfast was married to a man who was involved with the Irish College in Rannafast in the Donegal gaeltacht, but I don't think I really knew about that until I was a bit older.

My first real contact with the Irish language was at the Christian Brothers' primary school where we used to say the Hail Mary in Irish whenever the clock struck the hour. There were usually two classes in each large room, one taught by a Brother and one by a lay-teacher. The prayer was normally said by the Brother and we all answered in Irish, though I have to say it was just a matter of rote repetition of something we did not then understand. The Brothers had a name for being 'into' Irish, but in fact we learned very little Irish there. I found that students from Rosemount had more Irish entering St Columb's College than I had. Mind you, I remember us trooping into church to listen to a sermon in Irish on the feast-day of either St Patrick or St Columb. The fact that we did not understand it was not too important. The main thing seemed to be that Fr John Doherty was speaking to nationalist Catholic Derry in our own language. That was sufficient.

The Derry Féis, the annual cultural festival, had something of the same ethos. Almost every singing competition had one compulsory song to be sung in Irish and for most of the competitors this meant many hours of boring repetition of words and syllables that meant nothing to them. Since interpretation of the song gained marks, it was necessary to learn when one should look sad or happy, or change the quality of one's voice to suit the meaning, whatever that might be. I recall listening to 120 young girls, including my sister Josie, all singing the same Irish song. The adjudicators then recalled a handful of them to repeat the performance and a winner was eventually chosen. Josie, who was a good singer, got a recall, which gave her a certain local fame, but she didn't get among the prizes. The story in our family is that she consumed a bag of toffees after her first performance, as she had not expected a recall. When she went on for the second time, her voice had lost some of its original purity – the toffees had seen to that! Family honour was satisfied at another Féis when the youngest in our family, Margaret, joined with two classmates to win the girls' trio competition.

My first learning contact with Irish was in St Columb's College. Our teacher for the first three years was Seán McGonigle. He was a well-organised and disciplined teacher, who was a firm believer in rote-learning of basic grammatical rules. We got a very firm basis for all our future Irish studies from him: I am still grateful to him for this. His teaching was supplemented in our last two years by a concentration on literary aspects of the language, under the tutelage of Dr McDowell, President of the College, who also encouraged us to speak the language together, as we walked around the College grounds in our free time. Some took his suggestion seriously and some didn't: I was one of those who did – something I have never regretted.

Notwithstanding the first three years of Irish study at St Columb's during which we read books in Irish written by Donegal authors from gaeltacht areas, I was surprised to hear from a classmate of mine at the time that he intended going on holidays to the gaeltacht – a place, he told me, where people spoke Irish all the time in their everyday life. This was news to me, but it was still going to be a long time before I would, myself, spend time in the gaeltacht. Nevertheless, I look back to that conversation with my classmate, about this magical place where people were speaking Irish all the time, as being seminal in my inevitable move towards becoming an Irish-speaker. I had really begun to enjoy Irish and was, I think, getting good at it, by the time I had reached my final year at St Columb's. After all the talking in Irish that some of us had been involved with in school, the oral test in our final examination was what we regarded as a 'dawdle' – 'no sweat' – a soft thing!

Irish took a back-seat during my first two years in Queen's University, but in my last year I brought two influential schoolbooks back with me from Derry – *Mo Dhá Róisín* and *Mo Bhealach Féin*: they formed the basis of my non-engineering reading during my final few months in Belfast and did, in fact, begin for me a total involvement with Irish that has never stopped since that time.

When I arrived in Manchester I discovered a kindred soul, Paddy McSweeney, in Metrovick. We signed up jointly with *An Club Leabhar*, the book-club which had recently been set up to promote reading in the Irish language. Irish became our normal means of communication, even though his southern dialect and my Donegal twang were not too mutually compatible. We both also had an active interest in music and Paddy was a good pianist.

I wrote to my brother to see if he would be interested in attending a summer-school in the Irish College in Ros Goill

– one of the gaeltacht colleges that catered for adults, rather than schoolchildren. I was so unsure of my Irish at the time that I wrote to the President of the College in English – something of which Dr McLarnon laughingly reminds me still, whenever we meet. Looking back, I see that query in English as a measure of just how far I have come along what I might call the 'Irish highway' since then. We enjoyed our first fortnight in the Donegal gaeltacht, though many would say that we didn't experience a full-blown Irish-speaking area until we arrived, some years later, in Rann na Feirsde and Gaoth Dobhair, two famous Donegal Irish-speaking areas.

I have little doubt that part of the attraction that Irish had for us was that it was strongly connected with Irish nationalism and such nationalism was, for most Northern Catholics, almost a guiding principle of life. That may now seem to be attaching too much importance to it: perhaps so, but that was how it seemed at the time. I suppose we were always unconsciously looking for badges and symbols of our own worth in our own country. The system in the North then did not help, with Catholics seeming to be forever condemned to a secondary position and the government colluding in that injustice. With a largely Catholic population, Derry had an abnormally high unemployment rate in those days and gerrymandering by the Corporation of the day was to ensure that the majority population would never get power in their native city. In such an atmosphere anything which would establish our worth was vital, especially if it did, like Irish, seem to belong exclusively to us and not to those who were determined to hold us down. An area where Irish was normally spoken implied a world of new values, unconnected with the dour severity of second-class citizenship – a place where freedom could flower. Residents of the gaeltacht areas of those days would have been surprised to find that they were so regarded, for theirs was a pretty poor life in material terms and they were taking us in as lodgers to eke out their sparse finances. For us, however, they were an important symbol of Irishness.

Whatever about the theory of it all, the practical result of that first gaeltacht visit was that I returned to Manchester a more fluent Irish-speaker, already planning to go back to some other gaeltacht region the following summer. In the meantime I had the temerity to take on an Irish singing class in the Manchester Gaelic League, where, as teacher, I was only a few yards ahead of the posse of students. They might not have learned much, but I did!

Paddy Sweeney and I started to subscribe to the University Irish journal, *Comhar*, which soon advertised its annual summer school, or *comhdháil*, which was to be held the next year in Teileann, in Donegal. I attended it and met people like Dónal Ó Móráin and Riobárd Mac Góráin of Gael Linn. As far as I remember it was there I joined their weekly pool in support of the Irish language. Gael Linn was a vibrant organisation that was beginning to let Irish people see that revival was possible and exciting. I became a listener to their sponsored radio programme soon afterwards. My radio-listening in Manchester, confined to Radio Éireann, convinced me that there was a real revival in things native in Ireland. I started listening to the *Listen and Learn* programme in which Aindrias Ó Muineacháin taught Irish. What he called Irish didn't quite square up with my northern notions about the language: his Munster Irish was a new animal and a strange one. Little did I know then that I would in the future be listening to my own children talking that way. But that was still far ahead!

I began to look forward to returning to Ireland to live. It happened in 1953 when I took the job in the Technical Department of the Electricity Board for Northern Ireland. Our job was to look after any problems that the District Engineers were either unable or unwilling to deal with. That included investigating system faults and co-ordinating maintenance technicians to repair cables or lines, testing protection circuits on such systems and, when emergencies left us any spare time, seeking and examining tenders for new equipment. Getting a phone-call at three or four o'clock in the morning, with a hurried request to come to Enniskillen or Derry immediately was one of the less pleasant parts of the job, but the independence one enjoyed in nearly every aspect of the work was wonderful for someone in his early twenties. I also signed-on at Queen's University to do research on a mathematical analysis of electrical machines, which involved taking measurements on some of the machines in the Belfast College of Technology, so my days were pretty full!

An interest in things Irish was something that one kept hidden in the EBNI since I was the only Catholic in our office, or, for that matter, in any of the adjoining offices. Many years later, discussing these matters with some of my Protestant colleagues, I was surprised to find that they thought I shouldn't have done that but should have been very open about such things. I still wonder about that. Catholics always knew that certain things were not mentioned in mixed Northern company in case one might offend one's neighbours. In those days, I had begun to attend ceilithe and singing classes in Cumann Chluain Árd, up the Falls. I had little doubt that my workmates would see such a place as a hotbed of republicanism, which it was not, though there were people of all political beliefs, including republicans, in regular attendance there.

I had become quite a fluent Irish-speaker by this time and actually joined a drama group, Aisteóirí Naomh Bríd, who regularly staged plays in the city. I have to say though that we sometimes had more people on stage than in the audience. I met Helen Vaughan there and she later became my wife, so I suppose one could say we were 'setting the stage' for bringing up an Irish-speaking family, though we had not yet realised that! Belfast in those days had an active Irish-speaking community, even if it was, so to speak, underground.

Any free time I had from the exacting duties of the Technical Department of the EBNI was given over to travelling in one of the gaeltacht areas of Donegal or Connemara. I really appreciated my new nearness to these exciting areas after my two years of relative isolation in Manchester. It was on one such trip that I first saw the Donegal island of Inishbofin, when I was looking for Irish and music in that part of the country. All I remember now is coming round a bend in the road at Machaire Rabhartaigh and suddenly, Inishbofin was there, sitting high and proud like a mirage on a calm glinting sea, with Tory island behind it in the distance. I knew immediately that I had to get out there. But how? I met a big overweight boatman near the harbour who offered to take me out for a fiver which was a fortune in those days. Even if I had had that kind of money I wouldn't have given it to him: there was something about the man that repelled me. Not at all pleased when I refused his offer, he turned away, mumbling something uncomplimentary.

I stood on the quay, accordion in one hand and a rucksack on my back, staring out at my dream. I could see a fishing boat nosing out of the island and pointing towards me, seeming to get bigger and bigger as I watched, until the engine was cut and it drifted sideways towards the quay. A fellow of my own age, wearing a peaked cap and holding a coiled rope in his hand shouted something to me and landed the rope expertly at my feet. He pointed to a bollard on the quay and I threw the loop over that. In a few minutes the boat was tied up and three islanders jumped off, leaving the one with the peaked cap to look after the boat. I shouted to him in Irish, asking if was there any chance of a lift out to Inishbofin, but he didn't answer me directly. He first wanted to know if I could play music for a ceilí and when I assured him that I could, he told me to come on board and welcome. He laughed when I asked him how much it would be. 'If you can play that thing,' he said, indicating my accordion, 'you can come for nothing and stay forever.'

Safely landed on Inishbofin, I was brought to the house of what I'll call the Queen of the island, a happy woman in her late sixties. She wouldn't hear of me staying with my new friend, as his home wasn't good enough for a visitor. Instead, she decided that I was to stay in her own cosy house and sat me down to the best meal I'd had in a long time.

At the hurriedly arranged ceilí that evening my first surprise was that there were men of all ages dancing, but no marriageable girls, only young teenagers and older women.

The men were the dancing stars: even in the Walls of Limerick and the Siege of Ennis, they were trying to outdo each other in complicated battering steps while the girls had a secondary role. My friend told me that the rest of the women were working over in Scotland and would only return at Christmas.

Sunday was to be Sports Day at Machaire Rabhartaigh, a big social occasion, when there would be music in every corner. The islanders made me promise I would pretend to the Tory musicians that I was a native son of Inishbofin, whose musicians seemed to have a complex about the superiority of the Tory players and saw a chance here to raise their own musical image.

The boat-trip on Sunday morning was glorious, with all of us dressed up and ready for the fray. Big crowds had been reported in Machaire Rabhartaigh and there was even a rumour of some literary visitor, but no details – just that he had written real books! As we jumped off the boat they shouted to me not to forget that I was an islander. On the quay, a smallish man, whom I thought I recognised, addressed me in Dublin Irish and kept me in chat as we walked. I continued in my new Inishbofin Irish and he told me that he had written material in Gaelic and a play called *Borstal Boy*. I felt pretty mean as I affected a surprised response: 'You must be Brendan Behan,' I said. He seemed not displeased that a real Irish-speaking islander should recognise him. A crowd gathered round Brendan, all of them inquisitive but friendly, until the grumpy boatman who had tried to stick me for a fiver when I first arrived pushed to the front and started to imitate Brendan's Dublin Irish, in the hope of turning the crowd against him. It was all done in fast, fluent Donegal Irish and the boatman clearly assumed Behan couldn't follow him. I felt real pity for Brendan, but I needn't have, for he did something then that I have never forgotten.

He turned to his tormentor and began to recite at tremendous speed what I think was one of the Fenian cycle stories, the words pouring out in such a torrent that you couldn't possibly distinguish one from another. The open-mouthed

39

boatman had no answer – not that Brendan left him any vocal space for that – and the crowd started to laugh, but not *at* Brendan – more *with* him now and against his mocker. The Behan flow stopped abruptly at last and with a curt, 'Sin Gaeilge duit', he turned and led us Bofin boys in triumph to the pub.

LIVERPOOL RESEARCH AND CEILÍ BANDS

The Queen's University external examiner, Professor Meek from Liverpool, was very interested in the research I was doing part-time in Belfast. He asked to have a word with me on one of his visits and offered me a research fellowship in Liverpool, at the princely figure of £1,000 per annum. I was delighted with the prospect of being paid in Liverpool for what I was doing at Queens without any financial reward. My salary from the EBNI at this time was only a few hundred pounds more than this, so I had no real choice but to cross the channel again and set up in Liverpool, under my new research supervisor, Jack Lynn from Belfast. It was the start of a whole new phase, both in engineering and music, but I wasn't to know that then. Apart altogether from my engineering research in the University of Liverpool, I even studied Old Irish for some time there with Welsh professor, Melville Richards.

My electrical engineering research began as a theoretical investigation of tensors in the study of electrical machines, but moved gradually to a more practical approach involving analogue computers. In those days, such computers were not so easily available as they later became, so I had to build my own. That was certainly a learning process! The Atomic Energy Authority at Risley, not too far from Liverpool, became interested in the simulation of fast reactors and I was eventually drawn into a Ph.D. Study of the stability of such devices. The point was that the Dounreay Fast Reactor was being built then in Scotland and there was some worry about a melt-down accident that had occurred in an American reactor of a similar type. My job was to set-up parameters for the new reactor, with a view to determining safe operating conditions. I learned a lot about control systems and system stability in the process and got the Ph.D.

about a year before coming to Cork, but I sometimes wonder if the United Kingdom Atomic Energy Authority really got their pennyworth out of it!

One of my top priorities, on reaching Liverpool, was to find where ceilí bands functioned in that very Irish city. I found lodgings in Score Lane, near the famous Rocket pub, where George Stephenson had run the world's first ever train. I contacted an Irish priest in the nearby Catholic church, who answered my Irish music query by telling me that he thought I should not associate with such people! For him, they were not the type for me. But I did discover, in conversation with him, where these unsuitable people were wont to gather for their rather unrespectable celebrations and I hot-footed it towards them that evening. It was one of the best moves of my life!

I met a fellow-accordionist, Terry Doran, in St Alphonsus' Hall, where there was a regular Saturday night ceilí that attracted a big crowd. He suggested that I should go to St Mary's, Highfield Street on the Sunday night. It was there that the Gaelic League held its weekly ceilí. One of the fiddlers in the Saturday night band, Kit Hodge, also played at St Mary's and she supported Terry's suggestion. I was welcomed on the following night at Highfield Street, where the music was a shade less formal than at St Alphonsus'. I joined Eamonn Coyne, Seán McNamara and Kit (fiddles), Séamus O'Connor (piano) and Paddy Joe McKiernan (drums) for my first regular Liverpool gig. At that stage there was no money involved – just sheer enjoyment.

I had for some months previous to this been toying with the idea of getting a full-size accordion. My own was a medium-sized 48-bass model, with a few slightly unhappy notes: it could not compare with James McPeake's machine or with the one Terry Doran owned. A London company, named Bell's, regularly advertised shiny new 120-bass models that could be bought on hire-purchase. I wrote to them and in what seemed no time at all, my new, bright red, Marinucci accordion was delivered to the door. What excitement! It was a joy to bring it to St Mary's for the first night, where its crisp, musical bass added a new dimension to the music – at least, I thought it did.

I spent a lot of time practising tunes on my new accordion and there was general satisfaction with it at the St Mary's ceilí. I had also begun to teach an Irish class there during the week. All in all, Liverpool was looking good, though perhaps my Liverpool University research was not getting the attention it deserved. The only snag, after a few months, was that my accordion seemed to be getting heavier and heavier! I used to get a bus to the centre of the city on a Sunday evening and then walk my accordion a good distance to Highfield Street. I was getting a bit tired of it all and seriously considered withdrawing from the Sunday night commitment to St Mary's, until Tommy Walsh came to me one night and told me that the Committee had decided I was to go on the payroll like the others. I was excited, more by their approval than by the money and my accordion got lighter and lighter with each succeeding week!

Liverpool had been a home for the Irish for a few hundred years and had many Irish clubs, including the Gaelic League, of which I became a member. I began to attend Irish classes in St Mary's, but the teacher there, Peggy Atkins, whose name will re-occur in the context of Irish music, insisted that I take over the class. She became a student in it, as well as taking on the job of piano-accompanist to our singing instruction. One of the exciting things about Liverpool – and indeed it had been true of Manchester, as well – was that a number of the people that I would meet at classes turned out to be sons or daughters of native Irish speakers. One such was Tommy Walsh, whose father hailed from the Connemara gaeltacht. It was refreshing to hear the father's fine Connemara blas after a lifetime in Liverpool. Tommy was a pillar of the Irish community then, regularly acting as MC at ceilithe and organising big Irish concerts, where native artists performed. I remember Kathleen Watkins coming to visit in our house then, as we lived near Tommy. Kathleen played her harp at a celebrity concert in St George's Hall and was a big success. I remember Tommy kidding her about her well-known boyfriend, a certain Gay

Byrne, who was already a star of English radio and television.

I was then fortunate to have become a member of the Liverpool Ceilí Band, with whom I played for a number of years and so I learned something of the general joy that ceilí music engendered. My later association with the traditional music group, *Na Filí*, means that I can claim some basis for the distinction I make between the function of a ceilí band and that of a group. Notwithstanding the criticism that many, including the late Seán Ó Riada have made in recent years, of ceilí bands, I remain a staunch afficionado. Most of their critics have never been members of real bands, playing for dancers. Ceilí bands should not be compared with the modern Irish music groups, whose job is to play for listeners. Ceilí bands are for dancing to, and if you have ever played reels at speed in a good band for dancers who make the floor pulse in sympathy with the lift of the music, you won't need to be told what a satisfying feeling it gives. The empathy between good dancers and a top-class band is one of the magic pleasures one cannot explain. A good ceilí band doesn't just suddenly appear – it is, more often than not, the result of years of involvement by its members in other groups. That was how it was in Liverpool.

The seeds of my own appreciation of bands were probably sown in my youth, when I discovered in my Aunt Maggie's house that an accordion could make wonderful music. I remember, years later in Manchester, being in awe of the dance music two friends of mine could coax from their accordions in the Gaelic League band that played for our ceilí on a Sunday night. One of the accordions was offered for sale, just before I left to return to Belfast, and I bought it, not realising at the time, of course, that the die was thereby cast and I was about to start my long association as an accordionist with various ceilí bands.

Cumann Cluain Ard, in Hawthorn Street, Belfast, used to hold a ceilí every Sunday night, with Séamus Mallon, a well-known Falls Road character, as *fear a' tí*. Music was provided by one or two fiddlers, who asked me to vamp for them on piano. After a few weeks, a new band was brought in – The McPeake Family – which included old Francey and his son Francey on pipes, with James on accordion. They asked me to continue vamping on the piano, until James discovered that I had an accordion at home. He insisted that I bring it with me the following Sunday and from then on I ceased being a vamping pianist and became a real live ceilí-band accordionist. James and I had a great time, bluffing or vamping the tunes that the pipers would play, when we didn't know them, but our repertoire gradually increased.

Another important part of the proceedings was the swapping of jokes, for James had a great sense of humour and a fund of yarns. Our vulgar accordions belting out dance music must often have drowned out some fine pipe-music, but we did not know any better at the time, and the dancers seemed happy enough. There were many pauses in the programme of dances, to allow solo singers to come forward. The songs were all in Irish of course, as was everything in Cluain Ard. I was pleasantly surprised to find that I knew many of the songs from my youthful attendances at the Derry Féis. At least one solo by the two pipers, accompanied by Séamus on harp, was always a feature of the evening. They produced a beautiful sound in those days, long before they had become famous internationally as the first *McPeake Family Trio*. I have little doubt that this contact with uilleann pipes must have influenced my own decision, years later, to take up that instrument.

At one stage, we added on more instruments to the McPeake Family Band to make up a ceilí band that would enter a competition in the Belfast Féis. Winning must not have been our first priority, as I don't remember much about the result, though I think we did come first in the competition. The main result of it was that we got a booking to play for a ceilí in St Mary's Hall. I had hit the big-time at last and got five shillings (25p in today's money!) for my night's work. We put a lot of work into practising for that ceilí: I have an awful memory of old Francey McPeake insisting at rehearsal that we each play the tunes solo. I still burn inside thinking of my own embarrassment as I stumbled through a new reel that I had never got down to learning properly. I was alright with the band, where I could look good and not interfere with the general flow of the music, but playing solo was another matter entirely. My subsequent commitment to getting tunes exactly right – and not just there or thereabouts – stems from this incident. Perhaps there may be some consolation here for my uilleann-piping students, whom I sometimes make suffer for my earlier sin!

At the time of joining the Liverpool Ceilí Band, I also joined the church choir in my local parish, and was surprised to discover that the choirmaster, Tom Harding, was a fiddler who played in some of the bands. We played some tunes together and he invited me to be substitute accordionist with the Liverpool Square Dance Band. That was a new experience – playing Playford tunes, as well as Irish and Scottish music for English folk-dancing. I even learned how to play *God Save the Queen*! Eventually I became the regular band accordionist and we travelled a lot in the North of England and Wales, mostly playing for the English Folk Dance and Song Society. I remember a dance in North Wales where we finished up, as usual, with the British national anthem, only to have a girl jump up on stage and play the Welsh anthem on piano. Tom and I joined her music, as we were the only two in the band who knew the tune. I had recently learned to sing it, Welsh words and all, as part of a Welsh language course I was involved with in Liverpool. The Square Dance band brought me into contact with different people and different functions and a particular pleasure was playing for autumn barn dances in authentic big barns, with bales of hay and straw all around us.

I played solo accordion for both English and Scottish folk-dancers in their separate societies in the University of Liverpool and we sometimes travelled to other centres, like Leeds, for festivals. The local branch of the English Folk Song and Dance Society, with Ethel Anderson at its head, held weekend courses for dancers and musicians, where

46

guest speakers like Beryl Marriot, a top-class musician and dancer, taught musicians about playing for folk-dancing. She was an inspiring teacher. I remember attending one of her weekend courses, where she kept emphasising the importance of good, off-beat lift in dance music. I found it an interesting approach and was determined to employ it in my own playing. Imagine my surprise on the Sunday night in Highfield Street at our weekly ceilí to discover, as I came in late to the hall, that our fiddlers were playing in just that fashion – and always had! Nobody had ever talked to them about up-beat theory or about other useful playing gimmicks. They just played as they had always played, and it was the right way – the way that made dancers spring from the floor in the sixteen-hand reel. I learned yet another lesson that evening.

As time went on, I got invitations to join other bands and groups. Sometimes I would play five nights a week at dances throughout the city and its suburbs: from Bootle to Scotland Road and from Huyton to Aigburth, the Irish kept coming together to dance. I played for a while in the Shamrock Club in Lime Street for a different type of dance – one that included waltzes and quicksteps as well as ceilí dancing. The customers were not the kind of semi-idealists you could meet at the Gaelic League, but were, in the main, recent emigrants, including many nurses, who were just interested in a good night out and the chance of meeting other Irish people. My repertoire broadened to include new numbers like *Who's Sorry Now?*, in the company of Bob and Marie McNichol. Bob, who played fiddle, hailed from Mayo, and Marie, on piano, was Liverpool-born. The steamy hall was always packed and there was not much time for relaxation between numbers. It was real professional work and the money, as far as I can remember, was a bit more than one would get at a standard ceilí.

I remember playing one weekend with Kit Hodge for a dancing competition at Maureen Bolger's Dancing School across the Mersey in Rockferry. We started planning a Liverpool branch of the Comhaltas on our way back in the train that went under the river. It was a completely undemocratic process, with Kit appointing me as Chairman and herself as Secretary, with instructions to write to the Dublin head-quarters of the organisation for an application form. We nominated various musicians as a committee and presto! the new Branch had come to life. We used to hold regular monthly meetings in Peggy Atkins' house in Waterloo, where there was little business conducted but plenty of music played.

When Helen and I married, we set-up house in a Liverpool suburb called Huyton and I can remember at least one Comhaltas meeting taking place in our house, but that might just have been a separate celebration. I think that was the night Éamonn Coyne soothed our new baby Nuala on his shoulder when she cried. My memory says that Éamonn was still playing the fiddle as he walked around the room with Nuala on his shoulder but Helen says it didn't happen like that. I don't know whether to believe myself or not!

The first real participation of our branch in a Fleá Cheoil was in Longford when Kit, Mick Quinn, Seán Murphy and myself entered the quartet competition. The organisers did not know what province a group from England should enter, so they put us into the Connacht section, which, to our surprise, we won. On our train journey from Dublin to the Fleá the ticket-collector seemed very inter-ested in our instruments and in the fact that we were going to the Fleá to play music. He took a loan of Seán Murphy's mandolin and played a very appropriate reel – *The Long-ford Collector*. It was only then that we discovered he was a well-known performer, Noel Strange, whom we had the pleasure of getting to know well in later years.

The atmosphere at that weekend was something we had never before experienced. We started to play a few tunes on the street in Longford before a crowd that just kept growing until it had completely blocked the street. We were enjoying it until we saw two Gardaí making their way through the crowd. I said to Kit: 'We'd better stop.' 'Not at all,' she said, 'just keep playing.' When we had finished the tunes, one of the Gardaí asked us, rather officiously:

'Where are you from?' When we said we were from Liverpool their whole attitude changed. 'Stand back,' they shouted to the crowd. 'Give them room: they're from Liverpool!' Old men on the edge of the crowd started dancing to our music. Those early Fleadhanna were like that, before the folkies and the rockers discovered that Whit weekend meant wild Irish music. Fortunately, that stage passed and the Fleá got back on to an even-keel again. But the first fine rapture of the Longford Fleá remains in the memory.

I think it was soon after that that we decided to form the Liverpool Ceilí Band, not realising then how famous it would become. In the beginning it was just a band to enter the ceilí band competition at the Fleá. Nevertheless, we went to considerable pains to get a balanced line-up that would do justice to the Liverpool tradition. Some players were dissatisfied at being left out, but most of them realised that the omission concerned the balance of the band, so that it would give a good account of itself in competition. We had, in those early days, Éamonn Coyne, Seán McNamara and Kit Hodge on fiddles, Seán Murphy, a converted accordionist, on mandolin, Peggy Atkins on piano, Albert Crookshank on drums, and Kevin Finnegan and myself on accordions. I always enjoyed the driving energy of our playing, due in no small measure to the power unit of Crookie on drums, Peggy on piano, and Kevin and myself on accordions. We entered a few Fleadhanna and did well, but, like so many organisations and projects I have been associated with, the band only became really good after I left. I remember being surprised at how fine it sounded at the first Fleá after we returned to Cork and I told them they sounded just as good as the *Tulla* or the *Kilfenora* bands – which they did. When I was playing, I had not realised what a completely satisfying traditional sound the complete unit possessed. When they went on to win the All-Ireland and Oireachtas first prizes and made a few long-playing records, their continuing fame was assured. Being an ex-member of the Liverpool Ceilí Band was no small achievement then!

49

STILL LIVERPOOL!

Celebrity concerts were an important part of the exile's life in Liverpool. For many of the older second generation Irish, it was a welcome look back to their native land. It had been the same during my years in Manchester, when some well-known Irish singer, and perhaps a comedian, would come over around St Patrick's Day. They might or might not be accompanied by a musician. I remember Dermot O'Brien coming over in the days when he was equally well-known in the sporting and musical worlds, and Mary O'Hara, complete with harp, captivating hearts in the Gaelic League in Manchester.

In my time in Liverpool, the concerts were held in either the Philharmonic Hall or in St George's concert hall. There wasn't really any common denominator linking the artists who would be asked to appear in Liverpool, except their popularity. I remember names like Eileen Donaghey, Joe Lynch, Albert Healy, Paschal Spellman, Seán Ó Sé, Kathleen Watkins, Bridie Gallagher and Dermot Troy. Before my time, famous names like Josef Locke and Belfast tenor James Johnston topped the bill. Seán Ó Síocháin was a popular artist who appeared at a concert in St George's Hall in which I played a memorable part. Let me tell you the story.

Seán Murphy and myself used to play music for Maureen Bolger's dancing school in Rockferry. When she needed male dancers to make up a large troupe, she conscripted Seán and myself to be a part of her team. We couldn't equal the expert dancing of our female partners of course, but we were neat enough in our own way, and certainly passable in dances like eight or sixteen-hand reels, which was what we were to do on the stage of St George's Hall, in front of a capacity audience. Seán Ó Síocháin introduced us, the music started and off we went. I spotted Maureen, our teacher, in the wings, nervously monitoring our performance, but we were well-rehearsed and it was all going smoothly until my feet went from under me and I landed on my behind on the slippery stage. The audience enjoyed it immensely – their laughter was a sign of that – and even though I recovered almost instantaneously to continue the dance without a hitch, right to the end, they were still laughing when we trooped off-stage. Maureen was furious, but not with me. The audience were her target – for laughing, when I might have been hurt! Seán Ó Síocháin kept reminding me of that night for years afterwards, every time he met me. But it wasn't the sort of occasion one easily forgets!

We had another concert in St George's Hall, at which the west Cork accordionist, Riobárd Dwyer appeared. He was booked for successive nights, both of which were an outstanding success. Peggy Atkins accompanied him on the first night, at which I was present. I was captivated by the fluidity and consummate skill of the accordionist's performance and by the great lift that Peggy's vamping gave to his playing. Unfortunately Peggy was unable to do the job on the second night, as she had another appointment and I was asked to fill-in for her. I was a bit nervous about it, so Riobárd came out to our house in Huyton on the afternoon of the concert for a few tunes, so that we could get used to each other's playing. He was one of the nicest people you could meet and we got on well. The concert was a great success, because Riobárd's lifty reel-playing made vamping for him very easy. As well as that, I didn't often get the chance to perform on a grand piano in front of a capacity audience. That was a wonderful experience.

That concert may have been one of a number we organised for the Irish Centre Building Fund – an organisation I was involved with in my last couple of years in Liverpool. While the city had always had Irish societies which held functions in church halls and, in fact, wherever they could find accomodation, a few people had recently come together with the aim of procuring a building which would reflect the importance of the Irish in the larger Liverpool community and would provide an umbrella, as it were, for the disparate Merseyside organisations. I think the idea was

51

due mostly to two individuals, Tommy Walsh and Fr Michael O'Connor, who called a meeting at which we elected a committee to investigate the possibilities. One of the early decisions was to set up a fund which could help to finance the project. Tommy became its chairman and I was vice-chairman. We had regular committee meetings in our homes at which we discussed ways and means. I remember a series of weekly fundraising ceilithe, with a free band that I helped to cobble together, and Tommy as MC. There was a prevalent feeling that the Irish were on an upward path at last.

Various possibilities for a Centre were investigated and turned down before the Committee was told of a wonderful building on Mount Pleasant, near the University and the Cathedral. We heard that it was elegantly decorated though it would need a lot of work, and that there was a preservation order on it, which did, in fact, give an organisation like ours a better chance of getting it. Of course it would be extremely expensive, we were told. That story had just begun to break as I was leaving Liverpool to go to Cork. The work of the Committee was about to go into overdrive towards the wonderful new Irish Centre that eventually emerged a long time after my Liverpool sojourn. As had happened with the Liverpool Ceilí band, the Centre began to really prosper only after I had left! Should I now be reading a message from these signals?

In the early 1970s, when I was involved with the highly successful traditional band *Na Filí*, we appeared in concert on this stage of the Irish Centre. For me it was a happy, if nostalgic occasion, meeting old friends. The centre itself was a revelation, with Tommy Walsh at the helm as Manager of a busy, effective organisation and the Irish enjoying themselves in twentieth-century luxury at last. I always remember a session that weekend in Seán McNamara's house. *Na Filí* were playing an air at the request of Peadar Finn, flute-player with the Liverpool band. When it was finished, Peadar said, sincerely: 'Wonderful playing, lads. If it was any better, it would be wrong!' That was a moment I like to remember.

I went over there in a hurry on another occasion to be guest-speaker at the Annual Dinner when the programmed speaker, Seán Ó Síocháin, was taken ill suddenly. It gave me a chance to tell my story about Seán and the St George's Hall concert where I fell on the stage. Since everyone had been looking forward to a song, as well as a speech from Seán Ó Síocháin, I had to oblige with *Sweet Kingwilliamstown*. Imagine my surprise when I discovered that the chief clerical guest was from the very town I sang about – Ballydesmond, to give it its modern name! The Centre has had its ups and downs since then, but is still there, doing a good job for the Irish. My very last visit to it was as piper/singer with the Comhaltas Tour of Britain Group in 1995.

On that occasion I was asked to say a few words about the Centre, where we were playing. I said it was a place where I saw ghosts – ghosts of many musical friends in Liverpool. I remembered Paddy Joe McKiernan, singing in the home of fellow-musician, Peggy Atkins. He always sang the same song, with such feeling that it would break your heart. The song was *The Shores of Amerikay* – one that had always seemed to me a bit over-sentimental, but not after hearing Paddy Joe sing it for the first time. His people were all from Leitrim and he'd often talk about his feelings for Ireland and, in particular, his family's home county. It was at times like those that one could understand the intense depth of feeling that the second-generation Irish in Liverpool had for their native land. Paddy Joe's song satisfied a need that so many of them felt.

Another ghost of that evening was, of course, Peggy Atkins, a fine musician, who shared Paddy Joe's nostalgia for Ireland. The two of them went back to live in Mayo at the end of their lives, where we visited them a few times. Peggy's sister Ronnie, always a charming hostess at the Comhaltas meetings in their house in Waterloo, was married to Albert Crookshank, whom we all knew affectionately as 'Crookie'. He was the drummer with the Liverpool Ceilí Band, a position he grew into through his association with the Atkins family, for Crookie himself had no Irish background. This always surprised listeners to the vibrant

53

pulse of the band. I still have difficulty coming to terms with the fact that Crookie was one of my 'ghosts' that evening. I mentioned two others in the Irish Centre – big Seán Murphy, who used to play accordion beside me at the ceilithe in St James' in Bootle and who later was a valuable member of the Liverpool Band, on mandolin. Séamus O'Connor completed my list of 'ghosts': he was pianist in St Mary's, Highfield Street, in my earliest Liverpool days and used to attend my Irish language class there.

But that recent visit reminded me of other times. In our early days of marriage when we lived in Huyton, it was a good distance from town – an eightpenny fare on the bus, in fact. Coming back on the last bus from the Pier Head, I always had difficulty in making the bus conductor understand my Northern accent. I would say 'eight' and he would respond: 'You wot, mate?' I would repeat my simple request for an eightpenny ticket, to be followed by a repetition of his: 'You wot, mate?' Eventually, he would get the message and say: 'Oh! you mean *aight*.' One night, coming back from a ceilí, I decided to do something about the problem. As soon as I boarded the bus, I started to practise quietly to myself: 'Aight, aight, aight ...' in my best Liverpool accent. I think I had overtrained, though – when the conductor approached me, I lost my nerve and said 'seven', which meant I had to get off a stop earlier than Jeffrey's Crescent, where we lived, and walk all the way home, lugging my accordion. It proved to me I wasn't yet a native – not a real skouser.

I brought two visitors to Jeffrey's Crescent once when Helen was in hospital. They were Indian research students at Liverpool University, where I worked, and I thought visiting a semi-native's house might be of interest to them. My favourite menu – in fact the only menu I could guarantee from my kitchen – was scrambled eggs, so my two friends were treated to that. One of my master culinary strokes involved chopped onions in the scrambled eggs, to give the meal a little *piquance*, as the best French cooks would have it. Even though I say it myself, the meal was very definitely a success.

I visited Helen in hospital next day and told her about my visitors and the marvellous meal I had prepared for them. Helen was impressed, particularly when I mentioned the onions that I had blended in with the eggs. 'So you bought onions,' she said, 'that was a good idea.' I didn't want to take too much credit for the success of the evening and knew I should acknowledge her own contribution. 'No,' I said, 'I used the onions you had in the press. They were a bit old, but alright.' Helen informed me that she didn't have any onions, even old ones, in the kitchen press. Further investigation by her revealed that the 'onions' were actually hyacinth bulbs that she had intended to plant! I kept a close eye on my Indian friends for a few days afterwards, but they still seemed quite healthy!

About this time, too, I went, on Helen's recommendation, to the pictures, to see one of the big cinema epics that were so popular in the late 1950s and early 1960s. They all had similar kinds of titles: *Sodom and Gomorrah, Caesar and Cleopatra*, and so on. Maybe Helen meant it to be a rest for me, after my recent intense culinary efforts. I attended an afternoon showing of *Samson and Delilah*, I think, featuring Gina Lollobrigida, whose rather obvious physical attributes were a major attraction throughout the land. When I visited Helen in the hospital that evening she asked me what picture I had seen. 'Gina and Lollobrigida', I answered, not thinking. She has never let me forget it!

I am not surprised that Liverpool has had its fair share of comedians and quirky poets. There is an innate humour in the Liverpool air and they are always ready for a laugh. A friend of mine, a lady, used to play in one of the ceilí bands there in the 1950s. She herself told me this story. It seems that as well as playing her own instrument, the fiddle, she was often obliged to carry the band's bass drum to each gig. She did not have her own transport and so was dependent on the buses. She had the bass-drum in the bus-shelter with her and when the bus came she stepped forward to speak to the conductor, leaving the drum behind her in the shelter until she'd get the OK to take it on board. She meant to say to him: 'Will my big drum fit on the bus?', but in her confusion, what she actually asked him was: 'Will my big bum fit on the bus?' Quick as a flash came his answer: 'Turn round and let's have a look, love'!!

CORK AND KERRY –
AND THEIR GAELTACHT AREAS

It was in 1961 that I took up a job as lecturer in Electrical Engineering in University College Cork. There were academic connections between Liverpool University and UCC and, in fact, a former Liverpool academic, Professor Fred Teago had been in charge of the relatively new Department of Electrical Engineering in Cork before the appointment of Professor Charlie Dillon, a few years before I arrived. Charlie, a UCD graduate, had been a top engineer with ASEA, a big Swedish electrical company. When I settled into Cork, I discovered to my surprise that my former Belfast professor, Percy Burns, was doing some part-time teaching in electrical engineering in Cork too. Why would I not feel at home in the new Department?!

One of the most attractive things about our move to Cork was that I discovered, on reading the UCC calendar, that there were three professors of Irish there, as well as a thriving music department under Professor Fleischmann, with, to my astonishment, a lecturer in Irish Music. He was Seán Neeson, a Northerner who had once been Carl Hardebeck's secretary, and was then Cork Corporation lecturer in Irish Music at UCC. It seemed that two of my main interests in life, Irish language and music, were to be well served by this new beginning.

Having come from Liverpool in the swinging sixties, Cork and its University seemed just a little conservative. A summons to the President's office in my first week made me realise that the aforesaid swinging sixties had not yet reached UCC. The president, Dr Harry St J. Atkins welcomed me and asked me to sign a large book that had something to do with my university statute and conditions of employment. I read the paragraph I had been requested to sign regarding my non-interference with the morals or religion of the students. I laughed as I signed and said: 'I don't think I'll be doing any of that sort of thing.' Harry St J. Atkins, never noted for his humour, looked at me and said, matter-of-factly: 'Well, we'll sack you if you do.' Goodbye Liverpool; hello Cork!

My double life of engineering and music really began in Cork. I remember sitting-in on First Arts lectures in music during my first year there. We were a small class of half-a-dozen or so who did Harmony and Counterpoint with Professor Aloys Fleischmann, and Irish Music with Seán Neeson. Seán's lectures were mostly devoted to a modal approach to the subject and much of his time was taken up in class with transcribing modal settings of Irish folk-songs, which we copied, but it was Professor Fleischmann who guided us through the basic rules of musical composition. I had not signed-up officially for the course, so I did not take any examinations. They came some years later, when I registered as a member of the First Year B. Mus class in 1968.

My interest in old Irish continued for a time at Cork when we moved there, firstly with Professor Séamus Caomhánach of UCC's Irish department and subsequently with my good friend Pádraig (later Professor) Ó Riain. Séamus Caomhánach and I always spoke Irish together, which I considered a mark of approval of my Irish: I knew a number of fluent speakers who tried in vain to get Séamus to talk to them in Irish and became quite bitter about it when they failed! Séamus would often drop into our house for a Sunday evening chat, particularly after his wife Rosario died. What a storehouse of knowledge of the language disappeared when Séamus himself passed away.

We became part of an organisation for Irish-speaking families in Cork called Na Teaghlaigh Ghaelacha. There were probably a few dozen such families in the city at the time and we would meet for outings or to hold a Christmas party for the children, usually in Dún Laoi, on the South Mall. One of my jobs was to go to the Munster Arcade late on Christmas Eve each year, to pick up a certain red costume for a certain individual to wear that evening. It might even have been me, at times – but that was all a well-kept secret then, though some of my own children were not fooled. I remember one of them telling me that she recognised my hands as I gave out the presents! You can't win.

I was closely involved with setting-up a small Irish-speaking community in 1966 in Glanmire on the outskirts of Cork city. We formed a Company, Buaic Teoranta, which bought land and sold sites to Irish-speaking families who wished to build there. We still live in Ard Barra, next door to an Irish-speaking secondary school, Coláiste an Phiarsaigh, that our children attended. Looking back now, when Nuala, Úna and Niamh are all reared, how far away pre-war Derry seems, with our nationalistic yearning for things Irish – a goal we probably thought would never be realised, however much we desired it.

I was in a good position to compare the two Electrical Engineering departments of Liverpool and Cork from the inside as it were. Cork got most of the kudos, in my book, as the students were of a higher standard than in Liverpool and the level of Cork mathematics was superior. My assessment was later confirmed by a Liverpool professor who acted for a number of years as external examiner for the National University of Ireland (NUI).

One of the most inspiring aspects of UCC was the quality of a long succession of post-graduate students I had there. The very first of them was Steve Stott, at present Dean of Information Sciences in Hatfield Polytechnic in England, for whom we got unexpected financial support from Hawker-Siddeley, an English aeronautical company who were interested in our work in Adaptive Control. On a recent American tour I met two others who are doing very well in the top echelon of the electronics industry – Joe King and Ronan Ryan. I can add Ray Coughlan and Conor Downing, who are now lecturing in the Cork Regional Technical College, to my long list of research students from whom I learned more than they ever learned from me. Just to be associated with their academic development was a privilege that I have always appreciated. Talking of privilege, let me make it clear that, in my opinion, University life in itself was a privilege that none of us really deserved: we were just lucky to be doing a job that was so satisfying and stimulating. Continuing contact with the freshness and directness of youthful minds was a real bonus.

Strange to relate, one of our first big discoveries in Cork was Kerry – in particular West Kerry and the gaeltacht area of the Dingle peninsula. In the summer of 1962 we went on holidays to Baile an Mhúraigh, near Feochanach, to stay in the house of Jack Sé and his family for an unforgettable holiday. Nuala, our first child, was just a year old. We found what seemed to us a miniature paradise, where a new form of Irish was spoken and songs we hadn't heard before were sung. We had fresh salmon from the nearby river for lunch, or perhaps in a cold salad in the evening, when we returned from our wanderings. The Sé family completely spoiled us, of course, as we were the first paying guests that they had ever taken-on. We were originally due to stay with their cousins, but there was a mix-up and we were re-scheduled to Jack Ó Sé.

We used to play cards with them in the evenings and Jack would sometimes sing. I have a special memory of his rendering of *An Cailín Deas Rua*. Once or twice they had dancing, particularly when 'An Máistir' Mac Gearailt, i.e. the local teacher, would be there to act as MC and keep us all on an even keel in the Kerry sets. Jack was a bit of a seanchaí, or storyteller, though he wouldn't have made any claims to that himself. I wrote an article for Diarmuid Ó Murchú's magazine, *Agus,* when we returned to Cork, based on Jack's stories about a nearby broken-down castle called Túr Bhaile Dhá. It was in the Ó Sé household that I first met Muiris Ó Cuinn, a fine box-player, a gentle man and a singer of songs. It was from him that I got one version of *Rachad-sa 'smo Cheaití*, probably the most popular song in the sean-nós tradition of the area. Jack's daughter Peig and his wife saw to it that we were treated like lords on that first visit to Kerry.

There was a summer course in progress in the local school that summer, run by three people from Cork whom we were to get to know very well in later years. Séamus

60

Ruiséal worked in those days for the ESB, later became a teacher and editor of the Gaelic League journal *Feasta*, and is now my next-door neighbour: Risteárd Ó Murchú, whom I shall always remember for his inspiring singing of *Máirín de Barra* and who was a teacher in the school our children would attend in years still to come – An Mhodh-Scoil: and the third, Séamus Lankford, from a family well-known in Cork for devotion to things Irish, is still working away for Conradh na Gaeilge in the Árus in Cork's Mardyke, as is Séamus Ruiséal. Another Corkman there that year was Tadhg Foley, who was related to people in the area. He was one of Cork's real characters at that time. I remember him coming into our house in Cork subsequently when we were having a musical session. By way of introducing himself to the assembled company, Tadhg did a double somersault across the diagonal of the room, before giving his well-tried imitation of trombone-playing to an audience that was still settling after his shock entrance. One would always know when Tadhg had arrived at a party!

Our second visit to the west Kerry gaeltacht was to Dún Chaoin, to the house of Lisa Bean Uí Mhistéil in Ceathrú. Lisa's house was just up the road from Mailí Ní Chonchubhair's hostel. Lisa was Seán de h-Óra's sister and, if anything, an even better singer than her brother, who had made many recordings and was regarded as the doyen of the west Kerry traditional singers. It was a rare pleasure to hear her sing *Dónal Óg*, a song of the unrequited love of a poor girl for a high-born lad who, according to the song, could have had the daughter of the King of Greece as his bedmate – iníon Rí Gréige mar chéile leap' agat. Lisa's sensitive approach to this marvellous song of nature and of love, mixed together as they so often are in the Irish tradition, made us realise how privileged we were to have landed in Ceathrú. She looked after Nuala and Úna when a group of us went out by currach, or naomhóg, to use the Kerry word, to spend a day on the Great Blasket and see evidence of what had once been a closely-knit native community, with a proud literary tradition. Tomás Ó Criomhthainn's *An t-Oileánach*, *The Islandman*, Peig Sayer's *Machtnamh*

Seana-mhná, Recollections of an Old Woman, and Muiris Ó
Súilleabháin's *Fiche Bliain ag Fás, Twenty Years a-Grow-
ing,* assume an even greater importance when you are in
touch with the houses their authors grew-up in and when
you can talk to people who either knew them or were
related to them.

It was in Lisa's house that we first met a man whom we
never knew under any other appellation but 'Charlie'. He
was full of stories and perfect Irish and was a later com-
panion of Seán Ó Ríordáin, the Cork poet who derived
much of his inspiration from Kerry and, in particular, from
Dún Chaoin. We would sometimes go to the local pub to
meet 'Kruger' Kavanagh, the brother of my UCC colleague,
Séamus Caomhánach, and I think it was on this visit that
we first came across their sister Peig, from Baile Mór. It
would be hard to imagine members of a family more different than these three: Kruger of the extravagant, outgoing
personality – the man who claimed to have made it big in
Hollywood; Séamus, the studious academic who had spent
years in America and Germany; and Peig, their quiet,
welcoming sister.

In later years we spent very pleasant holidays with
other cousins of the Ó Sé family with whom we had stayed,
that very first year, in Baile an Mhúraigh – muintir Shé in
Ard na Caithne and subsequently, Bean Uí Shé in Baile an
Éanaigh. Dónal Ó Cathain, owner of the pub in Ballyferriter, or Buailtín, as the town was known locally, had become
almost our unpaid holiday agent in Kerry. We would ring
him in early summer and he would find us a place to stay,
especially a house that would welcome young children and
music. We even stayed one year in his own place, so we were
at the hub of all the singing and music, for Dónal's pub in
those days was a centre where music was not just tolerated,
but warmly welcomed. It was in his pub that I first met
Séamaisín Firtéir, his neighbour, who turned out to be a fine
singer, and from whom I learned a few good songs that I still
sing. I never hear the song *An Goirtín Eornan* without thinking of the first time I heard him sing it in Ó Cathain's.

Mícheál Ó Gairbhia and Seán de h-Óra were two others who used to frequent Dónal's pub.

Even when the session was over, Dónal had a nice way of arranging that we would continue the music in someone's house. A night listening to, among others, Mícheál de h-Óra, as he sang *Táim-se sínte ar do thuamba* was memorable. The song itself, with its profound pathos, always reminds me of the deepest music of the Flamenco tradition, but it was the strength of feeling in Mícheál's performance, rather than the music itself, which so impressed itself on me that night. I met another accordionist one night in Dónal's pub. She was Máire Ní Bheaglaoich, who reminds me whenever I meet her, that I taught her the reel, *Peter Street* that night. It was a good reel for accordionists, but pipers, including myself now, would not rate it very highly, partly, I think, because it is, as they would say up North, or in Scotland (where the reel itself began) *gie thran* (pretty difficult!) on the chanter.

An important visitor to the area in our early days was Seán Ó Riada, who rented Seán de h-Óra's house for a long period before he joined UCC in 1963. The Kerry singer was one of the first people Ó Riada brought to Dublin to record with Gael Linn in the days when it was still unusual for traditional singers to make records. Seán de h-Óra was a popular figure among both tourists and native Kerry people in those days. Everyone spoke well of him. The only criticism I ever heard was made by one or two singers who thought he interfered too much with the songs. I interpreted this to mean that they thought there was too much of de h-Óra himself in his singing. I don't think that criticism would be made anymore by critics listening to his records. I remember him telling me of songs and tunes of his that he thought had influenced Ó Riada a lot. It was not said in any boastful way – just a remark by a singer who knew that his tradition had importance. I often heard Seán Ó Riada talk about the Kerry singer with great affection.

An t-Athair Tadhg Ó Murchú was one of the most important people in the promotion of the west Kerry gaeltacht over the years. He used to be a teacher of Irish in

Farranferris College in Cork, the Diocesan seminary, but in addition to that, he ran a summer course in Kerry, firstly in a small hut, well known as 'An Bothán' and later, in the large building, now known as Brú na Gráige. Many priests of the Cork diocese were past-students of either the 'Bothán' or of Brú na Gráige. When I first met Tadhg, he had been shifted from Farranferris to become the curate in Carraig na bhFear, a few miles outside Cork city, which meant he had a correspondingly reduced connection with Brú na Gráige. Seán Ó Tuama brought me to Carraig na bhFear to meet him, at Tadhg's request. I was still fairly new at UCC and had just won a poetry prize in the Oireachtas literary competitions. The poem had been published in the Gaelic League journal, and it seems that Tadhg had been impressed by it. He wanted to meet me and his UCC contact was Seán, so the meeting was arranged. He was very kind about the poem and we became good friends. As well as doing his normal bit of mind-bending on me about the Irish language, he was very interested in the scheme for Irish-speaking families that we were setting-up in Glanmire. He came to Glanmire to baptise our youngest daughter, Niamh.

Tadhg was an unusual priest, always wanting to influence events for the good of the Irish language. He had friends everywhere who became, somehow, his arms of influence, whether in the University, the Church, or government, both local and national. His move to Carraig na bhFear inspired him to let everyone know of the Cork poets of the last century, since he was now in the middle of their territory. In no time at all he had President de Valera coming to his parish to open a monument to them, right in the centre of the village. He called it 'Fáiche na bhFilí' and it is still there to remind the parishioners in Carraig na bhFear that their area was once an important literary centre. I hope it also reminds them that they once had the famous Tadhg Ó Murchú in their ranks, as well as his namesake, Seán Ó Murchú na Raithíneach, one of the poets he commemorated. Equally, Brú na Gráige should be a reminder to the people of Ballyferriter and Dún Chaoin that a small, famous priest once walked their roads, trying to

Gaelicise the Irish clergy. He did a good job in Cork – a pity there were not more like him throughout the country.

More or less every summer in the 1960s we went to the west Kerry gaeltacht. I have to say that I regretted the changes that television was bringing to the area towards the end of the decade. Clearly, the people of the area had as much right as the rest of us to make themselves slaves to the box in the corner, but it was sad to see it squeezing out such a rich tradition. There was less time to talk and definitely less time for singing. Even Dónal's pub in Ballyferriter was changing and he knew it. I remember him telling me in the 1970s, when we didn't go there as often as in previous years, that it was Irish speakers like ourselves who, by their absence, were partly to blame for the disappearing songs and music. The days of Dónal hushing his customers so that everyone could enjoy *An Goirtín Eornan* or *Rachad-sa 'smo Cheaití* were gone. But television could not vanquish singers like Bríd Granville whose performances did not normally take place in the public arena, but in her house, where her husband Mikey always loomed large in the conversation, whether he was present or not! Her sweet voice singing a special song like *Dán na h-Aoine* could still roll back the years. It would be most unchivalrous not to mention the good that Radio na Gaeltachta has done, not only for singing and music, but for the general morale of the people of every gaeltacht area in Ireland, including Kerry.

Perhaps my greater involvement with the traditional group *Na Filí* in the 1970s was one of the main reasons for our less frequent visits to west Kerry. I remember us playing there once or twice, but we had so much travelling to do, particularly in the summer, which was the high season for foreign festivals, that it was difficult to fit in everything. I like to think that we carried a little of the Kerry tradition abroad with us, whether it was in Seán de h-Óra's *Maidin Ró-Mhoch*, in *Dálaigh's Polka*, or in Séamus Firtéir's *An Goirtín Eornan*. What is indisputable is that I personally learned much about the Kerry tradition, particularly its singing, in the happy summers our family spent there.

I should not forget the west Cork gaeltacht, almost on our doorstep. We were frequent visitors to Coolea and Ballyvourney in our early days in Cork, whether it was to attend *Dámhscoil Mhúscraí*, the annual Court of Poetry held every year in *Cúil Aodha*, or a concert in the hall, where you might hear Paidí Thadhg Pheig singing in his inimitable way, or discoursing with his partner in the *Agallamh Beirte*, or perhaps Mikí Ó Súilleabháin singing. That was before the younger generation of Mikí's family, including Diarmuid, had begun to take the stage and well before Cór Chúil Aodha had become a stage item. It was there that Seán Ó Riada organised Éigse Martin Freeman, to honour the English collector who, before World War I, had saved a large number of songs in the area. They were subsequently published in the journal of the Folk Song Society in the early 1920s. I said that Martin Freeman had *saved* songs in the area, and time has shown that this is, in fact, exactly what he did. Some of the songs had completely disappeared from the area, before modern singers, as well as Seán Ó Riada, recovered them from the Martin Freeman collection.

The song *Aisling Gheal* is a good example. The first time many of us heard it was at that particular *Éigse*, when Seán played it on piano, to let us hear what kind of music Freeman had collected. After his lecture, people asked him many questions and made many comments. I thought the best of them came from a man who had travelled from Cork city with me that day. He was Mícheál Ó Ceallacháin, an excellent musician and conductor of the Cork Youth Orchestra. He merely said to Seán: 'Your *Aisling Gheal* was very beautiful – could you play it again, please?' Seán did so, and *Aisling Gheal*, first collected in the area some 60 years previously from the singing of an old woman, had been relaunched. It has since taken on a new life, but the hands and heart that let us hear it that evening in Cúil Aodha are stilled.

PIPES AND PIPERS;
CHESS, FISH AND PHOTOGRAPHY!

Mícheál Ó Riabhaigh came to Cork city from Dublin around the same time as myself – in the early 1960s. He was a civil servant, but more importantly perhaps, he was an uilleann piper, with an intense interest in Francis O'Neill, the collector of Irish music, who had been born in Tralibane. Mícheál eventually established a kind of annual pilgrimage of musicians to O'Neill's birthplace, where they played and danced just as people in O'Neill's time had done. O'Neill, one-time Chicago chief of police, had published a number of books on Irish music, including two famous volumes of tunes that traditional musicians in those days considered almost the source of their art. His book of 1001 tunes was their bible and chief reference source when correct versions of tunes were required. Mícheál produced many articles on the topic and I remember illustrating radio programmes with him, where we played some of the music O'Neill had collected.

In his early days in Cork city, Mícheál ran the Pipers' Club in Dún Laoi on the North Mall. As far as I remember, it met there on a Saturday night and began with a class for his young piping students. After an hour or so of that, there would be a general musical session, not confined to pipes, nor to any particular age-group. Mícheál, strapped into a big set of Taylor pipes, would be at the centre of things, controlling what was being played and who would play it. I would often go to that session.

It was in Dún Laoi, too, that *An Ciorcal Staidéir* (the study circle) held its meetings on Wednesday evenings. Diarmuid Ó Murchú was the chairman and prime-mover of that organisation, which used to conduct its meetings in Irish. The evening normally consisted of a lecture followed by discussion and it was a popular venue. I remember people like Seán Ó h-Urmholtaigh, headmaster of Bandon Grammar School, talking there, as well as UCC staff and teachers. Seán Ó Sé of *Ceoltóirí Cualann* fame was another talker (and singer!) at Dún Laoi. I even gave a lecture there myself on the revival of Hebrew, a subject in which I was very interested at the time. I wrote an article on the same topic for the Irish magazine *Comhar*, with Ben Yehuda's life as a centre-piece. Ben Yehuda, a pioneer revivalist in the early years of this century, had gone to live in Palestine, where he set up his Hebrew-speaking household long before the establishment of the state of Israel. I am sure Ben Yehuda's story had been partly instrumental in pushing me towards the establishment of the Irish-speaking area in Ard Barra, a few years later. It is only now I realise that Ben Yehuda's example was the touchstone for that.

It is just another example of a situation where you may think you are making a brand-new decision, only to discover – perhaps years later – that it was almost pre-determined, with little real choice involved. I see my decision to take-up the uilleann pipes as being something similar. It is true that I did go along and ask Mícheál Ó Riabhaigh about getting a few lessons from him to start me off, and he certainly recommended a couple of pipemakers to me. I spoke to Denis Crowley, brother of the well-known pipe-maker of earlier times, Tadhg, the man who had written a tutor for the instrument. Denis was not in good health at the time and he died soon afterwards. I eventually bought a practice-set from Moss and Alf Kennedy, expert Cork pipemakers, in Montenotte. The wood from which the bellows was made had come from the the garden of the house in Montenotte in which Sarah Curran stayed after the death of her sweetheart, patriot Robert Emmet. Moss was at pains to point this out to me when he gave me the pipes, so that I would know it was no ordinary set.

As I have said elsewhere, James McPeake and myself spent years playing accordions in the same band as the two Francey McPeakes, who were piping. That must have had its effect on me. Then, when I had returned to England, Francey McPeake asked me to collect a set of pipes from a pipemaker called Hamilton. I had them in the house for some time and I remember trying to get sounds from them with no great success. It was nevertheless my first playing experience of the instrument and must have had some influence on my decision to take-up the pipes in Cork, a few years later. I often visited Mícheál's house with my practice-set of pipes and was always welcomed with a nice cup of tea and cakes from his wife. Tunes I got from him included *Port Gordon*, *The Banks of the Suir* and *Garrett Barry's*. In those days, his children were small and would be going to bed when I arrived. I remember one of them, Eoin, pretending to play pipes with a couple of sticks across his knee. That same Eoin is now a grown man and an excellent piper. He is, dare I say it, even better than his father! Mícheál himself was always proud to acknowledge that fact.

I think it was the actual sound of the chanter that first attracted me to the pipes and I know the same to be true for most other pipers. I met one piper in America who had no Irish roots but who had seen an uilleann piper in a film and was so taken with the sound that he went back to the cinema every single day of the showing, just to listen to the sound of the exotic instrument. Of course he was hooked from then on and just had to get a set of his own. My attraction to the instrument was a slower burner than that, but just as pressing.

Apart from the tunes I got from Mícheál Ó Riabhaigh, I used to like trying out other ones I already knew from my accordion-playing. The jig, *Rambling Pitchfork*, had a special place in my affections, as my Uncle Patrick used to play it on the fiddle in Carnanban. My daughter Nuala remembers hearing me practise it when she was still a child in her cot in our first bungalow in Cork. It was a well-known jig, of course, but I think her memory of it says something about the number of times I must have played it, and played it, and played it! It was one of the early jigs Nuala picked up on fiddle. My mother, who played the fiddle herself, was happy to hear that Nuala was playing it too, for she had always intended that I should be a fiddler, like my grandfather and Uncle on her side of the house. The Gormans, friends of ours in Derry, had a small fiddle that my mother wanted to buy for me when I was young, but that never worked out, whether from our lack of money or for some other reason, I don't know. Some years ago, when Nuala was over in Boston, I tried to say something about my mother's view of piping and fiddling, in a poem called *Nuala's Fiddle*:

> In Boston, Mass.,
> My daughter fingers notes
> On a fiddle my grandfather played
> In Derry: her reels dance
> Along over-grown paths
> Once cleared by his bow.
>
> Deep in my father's grave
> My mother hid music
> That her children might not know
> She could draw a bow like the rest.
>
> A pity, she said to my playing,
> A pity we didn't buy
> Thon wee fiddle o' the Gormans that time,
> And you'd not be saddled now
> Wi' them oul' pipes.
> But I knew
> Chanter – like bow –
> Would clear its own path.
>
> Years cover-up the players
> But tunes remain:
> Old notes from a bow
> Re-form on pipes
> And echo on fiddle again
> In Boston, Mass.
> Chanter or bow is a baton
> To take for a turn
> And pass.

The first time I ever played pipes for the entertainment of others was in our house, when a couple of UCC friends were visiting. It was no big deal for them, of course, but as I played the *Coolin* in the way I remembered Francey McPeake play it, I knew I was travelling along a grand new road. I didn't know where that road was going, but I was very happy to be on it.

Apart from infrequent lessons in Mícheál Ó Riabhaigh's home, I had no other formal instruction on the instrument, but picked up what I could in the early years from people like Francey McPeake, Peadar Broe and Paddy Maloney, whom I visited a few times after Ceoltóirí Cualann's first concert in UCC. I remember being quite taken by Paddy's chanter work in the jig, *Sixpenny Money*, at that concert and I think my playing of it is still influenced by Paddy's style. Peadar Broe, a good friend of mine who lived in Fermoy, was an excellent piper, whose playing I first heard on the Claddagh record, *The Drones and the Chanters*. When I met him subsequently, he was keen that I should understand that the track he played on that disc was not at all representative of his best work. Having listened to his inspiring piping on many occasions in his home, I can testify to that fact. Peadar's tight style of chanter-playing and his facility with the regulators made him a superior model for an embryo piper like myself in those days. He enjoyed his spell as a student in the Music Department, after he had taken early retirement from the Army. His very presence in UCC was an inspiration to the other students. Peadar was a real traditional musician and made the subject live, as did some others who were there at the same time, namely Seán McKiernan (a fine piper from Connemara), Matt Cranitch (my colleague in *Na Filí*) and Peadar Ó Riada (son of Seán Ó Riada). I played pipes at Peadar Broe's funeral and thought it a great honour.

I remember Mícheál starting a class of uilleann pipers in the Cork School of Music. He was pleased that the institution was thereby giving approval to the instrument he loved. The first class really consisted of the best pipers from Dún Laoi moving some few hundred yards to the annexe of the School, situated in Wellington Road. With the support of the School of Music, Mícheál instituted an annual pipers' concert in the auditorium of the School, in Union Quay. Leo Rowsome, one of Mícheál's former teachers, played there a few times and *Na Filí* appeared in a number of them. My daughters Nuala and Úna and myself performed there in later years, with Nuala on fiddle, Úna on mandolin and myself on pipes. The MC at the annual concert was Mícheál Ó Murchú, otherwise known as *An Gabha Gaelach*, (the Gaelic Blacksmith) who would always introduce the event most formally and recite one of his own poems in Irish during the evening. Cáit Ní Chuis, the Limerick fiddler, was a regular performer, as was Con Foley and his traditional group, also from Limerick. Their music always had a distinctive sweetness. It was usual to adjourn, after the concert, to Dún Mhuire, at that time the Legion of Mary hall, on the Grand Parade, where there would be sandwiches, more music, chat and perhaps a tune from Mícheál. But those concerts came to an end surprisingly soon – when we attended Mícheál's funeral mass in St Joseph's Church, Mayfield in 1976, everyone realised that a unique phase of Cork life had passed away.

Bridget Doolan had, by this time, become Director of the Cork School of Music, succeeding Bernard Curtis. She asked if I would be willing to teach uilleann pipes in the School, which I readily agreed to do. I was a bit worried about how his senior students might receive me, for some of them were very good indeed, but they were pleased that the class was to continue. I suppose I had a slightly different repertoire to present to them, based on what I had been playing for years with *Na Filí*. Class membership changed over the years, but I have happy memories of sessions there at a certain stage with Rosaleen O'Leary, Angela Corkery, Mary Mitchell and Kieran Ryan, particularly when the formal class was finished and we just played and played. For me, they were inspirational students in an inspirational time. They probably did not realise that themselves! At another time I had two Diarmuids in the class, Diarmuid Grainger and Diarmuid Moynihan, as well as another in the distinguished list of Cork female pipers, Caoimhe Héarún, and, recently, Floraí Neff, a young piper of great promise. All are still playing excellent music – much better than their teacher, of course – and that is how it should always be. Teachers must continually strive to make themselves redundant, particularly when dealing with traditional musicians. The sooner the students start to sort out their own problems and seek other influences besides that of their first teacher, the better for their piping. Of course, it goes without saying that you, as teacher, do not claim any of the limelight if you produce a good student. It's enough that you have had the satisfaction of being witness to their musical growth. They must be allowed to fly free, like emerging butterflies in a sunny garden, landing where they will. Thus endeth the first lesson!

My first trip abroad to play Irish music occurred in the 1960s, when James McPeake rang from Belfast to know if I would go to France with himself and Hilary Galway, another accordionist, to play for dancers from the Tyneside area of England, who were to attend a number of Festivals with their director, Phil Conroy. It was there I began to understand the reason for the big processions these Festivals hold every morning. They are nothing more than ways of inveigling the audience in for the evening performance. Playing a heavy accordion under the hot sun of Dijon is no joke, particularly when it's all up hill and down dale, but we had good times there too. We were processing through a small French town whose name I did not even recognise, when, out of a group of old men sitting on a window-sill, a very senior citizen ran out to us and pointed to the tricolour we were carrying. 'Irish?' he questioned, and when I said we were, he looked into my eyes and said just one word – 'McSweeney'. I was bowled over to think that an old man would remember the Lord Mayor of Cork who had died on hunger strike in an English jail, all those years ago. We tend to forget that McSweeney's death was world news in those days. When I told the old Frenchman I had just come over from Cork, he was all smiles and handshakes. I tell you, I stepped it out proudly after that encounter!

I have spoken already about the Pipers' Club organised by Mícheál Ó Riabhaigh. It was not the only traditional music venue in Cork, as Comhaltas Ceoltóirí Eireann had a local branch then – Craobh Phroinsiais Uí Néill – which, in our early years, used to meet in the Group Theatre in South Main Street. Some of the musicians we played with there are long since gone: Sligo fiddler Dick Nangle, whistle/flute-player Ned Maher and his brother Paddy, flute-player Charlie O'Sullivan, Mick Millen, a very good fiddler from west Cork and many others. From time to time, players from other areas came to stay for a while in Cork. Two such, who gave a welcome fillip to our music, were Séamus Connolly from Clare and Ben Lennon from Leitrim. Séamus has been in Boston for many years – I met him there recently – and Ben has gone north again, just when the pair of us had started to enjoy a few nice sessions in our house in Glanmire.

We had a ceilí band in the Comhaltas branch, which sometimes competed at Fleadhanna. I still remind Matt Cranitch of the time we beat their family ceilí band at the Cork Fleadh in Killeagh. I think they made a better sound and were more precisely in tune than we were, but the adjudicators reckoned our group was a bit more traditional. Matt was a member of a stage group we put together once for a show, depicting, I think, emigration and, in the same show, a much younger Lena Bean Uí Shé was the love-lorn lass. Lena is nowadays involved with another Cork branch of Comhaltas, in Nemo Rangers Club, where they pay special attention to the training of young people. I met Dick Tobin there, another of the original Comhaltas people, when Lena, on her first visit to our weekly musical session in the Heron's Perch pub in Glanmire, asked me to come out to talk to the youngsters about the Irish tradition and play them a few tunes on the pipes.

The Heron's Perch session started about five years ago, when Tadhg Ó Loingsigh, owner of the pub, asked my daughter Nuala to get a session going. Nuala had just returned from America and was happy to get the opportunity to play traditional music, for that was what Tadhg wanted. I joined her on pipes and we kept it going for about a year, with the help of various other musicians and singers who would drop in from time to time. Then Nuala went to Galway and began to play fiddle with the street theatre group Macnas, while I continued the session. Various musicians came and went – sometimes I would be the lone player – until we now have a core-group of Charlie Healy on

74

concertina, Bonnie Shaljean on harp, Tony Canniffe on mandolin, Tadhg Ó Súilleabháin on bodhrán and myself on pipes. Another regular at our sessions, until he went back to America, was Bill Myers who, as well as being a guitarist and singer was the greatest expert I have ever met on computers and music. I miss him a lot. Most of the musicians, including myself, are also singers, but we also have regular singers like Mary Canniffe, Sinéad Cahir, Ann Merrick, Tom Mullins, Cliff Wedgebury, Tim Nyhan, John A. Murphy, Fionnbarra Ó Ceallaigh, Dónal Mac a' Bháird and the fear a' tí (the landlord) himself, of course, Tadhg Ó Loingsigh. We have even had storytellers, reciters of poetry, dancers, both solo and set and other unclassifiable entertainers. The only thing you can say with certainty about the Heron's Perch session on a Tuesday night is that no two weeks are ever the same.

My Greek teacher, Lydia Sapouna, was there one evening and we announced that I would sing a Northern song in Irish. In fact, it was a carefully rehearsed Theodorakis number in my best Greek, accompanied by the other musicians. She enjoyed it enormously and gave me full marks, but I wonder if some of our audience really believed it was Ulster Irish and therefore, by definition, almost unintelligible anyway! Lydia's father came another evening on a visit from Greece, and we perpetrated the same deception, though I think Lydia rather expected it this time. Her father Alekos, thought it was a marvellous evening and still tells his Greek friends about those wonderful Irish people! Every letter he sends has an enquiry about the singers and players of the Glanmire session, where we have complete strangers from all over the world visiting us, since news of the session made its way on to the Internet.

Charlie Healy and myself often have a Sunday night session in our house where we try to resurrect half-forgotten tunes, with a view to including them in our Tuesday night repertoire. To help other players join in with us at the session, we have a repertoire list that I produce on computer and which keeps expanding as we go. Notwithstanding that, I would not like to have a gun put to my head and be told to play a particular set of tunes from it, without rehearsal! Even though we regard this long list as our repertoire, I can't really claim to be up to scratch on it at all times, but it's a spur to keep learning! Since we always welcome other instrumentalists and singers at our session, the list goes some way towards putting them at their ease, if they want to join in.

The Heron's Perch session is the very first Irish music gig that I have ever been able to walk to and that's a new experience for me, after years of going by bus or car or plane or train. To decide, just three minutes before starting time, that I should pack my pipes and stroll down the hill from Ard Barra to the village of Glanmire, is a real luxury. What is nice about it too is that, as well as strangers who will be there, I'll meet local Glanmire people. The fear a tí, Tadhg Ó Loingsigh is one of a small committee of Glanmire people who formed a local body, Coiste Gnó Ghleann Maghair, a few years ago, with the avowed aim of improving the place. That is already happening, with social events, contacts with County Council representatives about practical improvements to the environment and suchlike being their on-going priority. Last year, Tadhg suggested to me that we should get together and sing a mass of mine in the local Catholic church. We managed to get a choir from the Heron's Perch, along with some of their friends, to sing the mass, which was celebrated by Canon Burke. In .1996, we sang the same mass on St Patrick's Day, with An tAthair Ó hIcí in the driving seat.

I had an earlier musical contact with the village about 20 years ago, when we formed a ladies' choir, Cór na Glaise Buí, for an Oireachtas choral competition. We sang some choral settings for which I had previously won Oireachtas prizes in the literary and music sections of the annual festival. Practising for the event was good fun and the trip up to Dublin was great, but we didn't win, being pushed into second place by the marvellous ladies' choir of St Mary's Dominican Church, Pope's Quay, Cork, with my very good friend Fiontán Ó Murchú conducting them. Fiontán was kind enough to say that we were doing the right thing by singing new, original music.

Chess was one of my passions in our first year in Cork. I had been introduced to the Cork Chess Club which met in the café of the Savoy Cinema in those days. But that was not enough for me – I had to join a postal chess club, which meant that I kept receiving their latest six moves from each of my six opponents and had to respond immediately by post.

One of my adversaries was a Church of England minister from near London, who revealed a more competitive edge than I had expected. We were involved in two games and I was ahead I one, while he had a slight advantage in th eother. I thought we might call it a draw in each of them and suggested this in a letter. I was shocked to find that he promptly accepted my offer of a draw in the game in which I was ahead, but said that we should continue the other game, as he thought that he could win! That's christianity at work!

When I had 'been there and done that' in chess, I turned to photography. I must have a very patient family, for they suffered having their kitchen turned into a darkroom, with only a minimum of complaint. They even professed considerable interest in the colour prints of themselves that I was turning out in the days before colour was the norm.

But photography went the way of so many other hobbies of mine (including beer-making!). I sold my enlarger and equipment and began to look around at other things. One of these was art – in particular, painting with pastels. My wife Helen has always been the artist in our house, with many fine paintings to her credit. She is also closely involved with the Maclise Art Society, named after the famous Cork artist of the last century. I suppose choosing pastels instead of oils, which Helen used, was one way of distancing myself from the competition. I had some lessons with Virginia Sandon, an excellent artist, who taught here, before she moved to England with her husband, Nick. She encouraged me to submit work to the Maclise Art Society. They turned one down, but exhibited a few others. I even had the temerity to submit one to the Pastel Society of Ireland, based in the North and I was not a little surprised when they hung it at their annual exhibition.

Even before we came to live in Glanmire in the mid-1960s, I was a regular night-visitor to the Glashaboy river, which flows through Glanmire village, patiently trying to capture one of the big white trout that swam freely there in those times. I still remember the excitement of the sudden splash in the darkness, when one had been hooked – but it was never on my line. Since we came to live here, I have not taken a rod on to the river-bank, not even when fish were said to be giving themselves up. Looking back now, I'm glad that I didn't catch any of those Glanmire sea-trout. Can you understand that?

NA FILÍ

It was in 1967 that Matt Cranitch and I were looking for a whistle-player to join us as a trio. In those days a group of us used to attend the Comhaltas Fleadhanna Ceoil and would enter competitions, mostly for the fun of it. In fact, all our playing in those days was sheer enjoyment, whether at a session in one of our houses or playing on the streets at a Fleá. Matt performed regularly with Réamonn Ó Sé in a group that a friend of ours, Paschal Ó h-Uallacháin, a great singer and pianist, used to run. They played a repertoire which was largely Carolan music and copies of Ceoltóirí Cualann arrangements. Paschal himself was deeply influenced by Seán Ó Riada's piano style and at many a session in our house in Glanmire he would 'do an Ó Riada for us!' I remember Seán Ó Riada's wife Ruth telling me once that herself and Seán were at a function where Paschal played the piano. Paschal did his Ó Riada 'thing' and both Ruth and Seán found it all very strange, even a bit uncomfortable – I think 'uncanny' was the word Ruth used in telling me the story.

Réamonn, who was studying for the B. Mus degree in UCC, gladly agreed to join us. We had a great time then, exchanging musical ideas and putting them into practical arrangements, so that we won various competitions, to reach the All-Ireland trio final in 1968. I have to say that many were surprised when we did not win it, the adjudicators commenting that we were too organised, with too much harmony!

However, we took the road again the following year and reached the All-Ireland final in Cashel. We had a different set of adjudicators this time, but I felt that we would get the same result if we played it our way again. My cowardly suggestion to Matt and Réamonn, just before going on stage for the competition, was that we should just bash out the music the way the adjudicators seemed to want it and forget about harmony and presentation. All three of us were aware, of course, that this course of action would probably gain us first prize.

I am glad to say that my colleagues insisted we play the way we had always done, and which we believed to be the right way. That year's adjudicators, who included the late Rory O'Kennedy of Dundalk, who used to have the Siamsa Band, and the famous John Joe Gardner, had a quite different view of our music, lavishly praising what their predecessors had decried. We won easily and I learned a lesson that day about sticking to one's principles!

I have always said that the year I won the All-Ireland in Cashel was not a great year for pipers, but a good year for adjudicators, who were, in fact, Willie Clancy and Willie Reynolds. They were very kind in their adjudication. That was the same Fleá at which *Na Filí* won the All-Ireland trio competition, which led directly to an invitation from Mercier Press to make a record. My friend Séamus Caomhánach from west Kerry was the person who recommended our name, *Na Filí*, as one that was Irish and pronounceable! There is a story to that as well: the first name we chose was *Na Fianna*, which seemed good, until I opened an evening paper one day in Dublin to see the picture of a group there who were called – yes, you've guessed it! – *Na Fianna*. That group had just produced their first record. We had already printed hundreds of publicity cards, with Réamonn, Matt and myself smiling out, above the name *Na Fianna*, in heavy black print. The photograph had been taken by a very good musical friend of ours, Dónal Ó Mairtín, who died recently. So it was back to the drawing board for a new name and new cards – just in time to let Mercier know that the name on the record should be *Na Filí* and the title, as suggested by Séamus Caomhánach, *An Ghaoth Aniar/The West Wind*.

It was at the suggestion of Séamus that we included a poem on the record sleeve:

An ghaoth aniar, bíonn sí fial The west wind is a generous
                                                        wind
Agus cuireann sí iasc i líonta, And fills the nets with fish.

Séamus always boasted that he was the one who had baptised our group. Others involved in the project were Loretta McNamara of Mercier Press, who had first mentioned the possibility, Paddy Hughes, who was producer and Norman Young, still a good friend, whose sound-studio in Cork's South Terrace we used for the recording. In those days, Norman engineered a number of records, both of music and speech. Paddy Hughes was keen on a certain amount of speech and poetry on our record – that's why I recited a verse of *Caoineadh Eoghain Rua*, while Matt played the air on fiddle.

One of the first letters sent out by *Na Filí*, after winning the All-Ireland competition, was an offer of our musical services to any group organising functions to assist those who had been displaced by the recent troubles in the North. We promised to do such concerts without fee and had responses from various groups. We played in the Bogside in Derry and in Belfast for the Bombay Street fund. It was an exciting time to be moving around the North and to experience such a warm welcome everywhere.

The record got some fine reviews – one of which led us to Liverpool and to a situation where the English folk-group, *The Spinners*, very big on the English scene in those days, were our backers. This is how it happened.

Tony Davis, leader of *The Spinners*, was at this time the editor of a Merseyside folk magazine, *Spin*. He wrote a very enthusiastic review, which was, I am sure, at least partly responsible for our subsequent successful appearances over the years at English folk-clubs and big festivals like Loughborough, Cambridge, Sidmouth and Inverness, as well as top-billing at the Albert Hall Folk Prom, run by the English Folk Dance and Song Society. Eric Winter and Fred Woods were influential columnists and journalists in those days, who happened to be fans of *Na Filí*.

I remember us being chief guests at the Spinners' Club in Liverpool on a few occasions. We were impressed by the group's friendliness and their willingness to take on a backing role on stage, for our final item. The warmth of the welcome we received from the audience was something I won't easily forget.

Speaking of club audiences in England, I remember our visit to the Watersons' club in Yorkshire as something special. It was on a Sunday evening, after the weekend of the Loughborough Festival. The Watersons and Martin Carthy were splendid hosts. Yorkshire audiences were well-known for telling it like it was and they didn't overdo the respect for artists – and that applied to their own home group, as much as to anyone else.

After one song, Mike Waterson walked to the rear of the stage, put a hand on the back wall and leaned his head on his arm, obviously deep in thought about his next song – consulting the Muse, as it were, while looking at the ground. His down-to-earth Yorkshire audience didn't go for that sort of posturing in their club, so a loud voice from the back seats broke the artistic silence with a question: 'Have anyone got a bucket?' The hall exploded in laughter and, to give them their due, the Watersons were not slow to see the funny side of it.

The performance of Réamonn Ó Sé, our whistle-player, at some of his university examinations was not, according to his professor, quite up to scratch, so he was called in for interview by the Head of the Music Department, professor Aloys Fleischmann. He was told very firmly that if he wished to get his final examination he'd have to concentrate on his studies and give less time to *Na Filí*. Poor Réamonn was distraught and decided there and then to give up his involvement with the group. He informed us of his decision and then went back to tell the professor that, as an earnest of his firm purpose of amendment, he had left *Na Filí* and would concentrate all his attention on the B. Mus. He was awarded his degree in music that year and we lost a fine musician.

When people ask me why Réamonn left *Na Filí* in the very early days of the group, I tell them that he really loved our music passionately, but was forced to resign, just to show the University that he was truly interested in its definition of music. That still rankles in my mind.

Réamonn recommended a friend of ours, Tom Barry, who was also a B. Mus student at the time as his replacement. Tom was an excellent whistle and flute player and took Réamonn's place in the group, remaining with us until we finally disbanded, many years later. One of our early commitments with the new group was the making of our second record, *Farewell to Connacht*. In those simple days one didn't spend weeks and weeks, planning and recording an album. Our second was actually done as part of a weekend visit to perform in a few Belfast clubs. The concerts had been organised by John McNally, the former Irish Olympic boxer, whose own group, *The Freemen*, included a very good friend of mine, James McPeake, one of the famous McPeake family of Belfast.

It was John who put us in touch with Billy McBurney of Outlet, a company that produced a lot of traditional records in those days. His artists included Seán McGuire, Rodger Sherlock, Joe Burke, Finbarr Dwyer, Séamus Tansey, Tom McHaile and many others. They got a lot of radio air-time, both here and abroad. His sound-man was Cel Fay from Dungiven. Over the years, I continued to keep in touch with Billy and Cel and was sorry to hear of Cel's untimely death a few years ago.

I'll never forget an incident that occurred on our first visit to the studio. Cel was setting up the mikes and put what he considered an adequate number of them around us. However, Matt was not happy with the arrangement for his fiddle. We had, a short time previously, returned from a session with the BBC in London, where Matt had been impressed by the placement of an extra mike, coming over his left shoulder from behind.

He explained very carefully to Cel what the BBC engineer had done. Cel listened patiently, saying nothing until Matt had finished. 'Hm ... m,' said Cel, nodding his head, 'sounds like a clever little so-and-so'; but he made no effort to change his own mike set-up! I think we played concerts on the Friday and Saturday nights of that weekend in Belfast and recorded all day Saturday and as much of Sunday as allowed us to drive back to Cork for our Monday morning jobs, having completed the recording. That, in fact, was the way it always was with *Na Filí* – we were confined to weekends and holiday periods for our trips abroad and to week-nights for Irish concerts and radio or TV shows.

It seems to me that there were more regular outlets for Irish music on RTE in those days. We were the resident group on a number of TV series produced or directed by Joe O'Donnell, Seán Cotter and Noel Ó Briain. Programme names I remember from those days were *Isteach Leat* and *Ag Déanamh Ceoil*. We would usually record a couple of programmes on a Sunday in Donnybrook. Seán Ó Sé, who has been a friend down all the years, would often be there too. I remember *Horslips* making their TV debut on one such programme, where we were the resident group for the series.

We would spend the early part of Sunday rehearsing and then record the show, or shows, in late afternoon, hoping there would be no serious mishaps that might cause the floor-manager, who was in constant communication with the producer upstairs, to step forward, waving his hands and calling for a re-run.

I remember the final tune by *Na Filí* on one of the shows: it was a nice set of reels – which were going just great until the bottom joint of my bass drone dropped off and the pipes let out a not very tuneful squawk. Luckily, the credits had come on screen and the increasing volume of the series signature tune covered my embarrassment. Weeks later, when the programme was shown on RTE, I took great pleasure in seeing what no one else had seen – the bottom end of my pipes plonking on to the floor, after another sterling performance!

NA FILÍ ARÍS

Our new record from Outlet, *Farewell To Connacht*, came out in August 1971 to considerable acclaim. Mary Hardy, folk-columnist with the *Irish Post* newspaper in England had asked her readers the previous week if they knew anything about 'these young men' that Tony Davis of the *Spinners* had been praising so lavishly! She wrote a very complimentary review the following week, after she had received the record, hoping that we would soon get over to London, which we did, when we played for various BBC programmes and in the Singers' folk-club, possibly the most famous in England in those days, with hosts, Peggy Seeger and Ewan McColl. About this time we played at a big Lughnasa Medieval Festival in Carrickfergus Castle, with the Pattersons, the chief Northern recording group of that time. Coincidentally, the foreword to our programme was written by another Patterson, who happened to be the mayor of Carrickfergus then. My chief memory of the event is that all the performers were dressed in long robes and carried wooden swords. I claimed that I wouldn't be able to play the pipes in such a get-up, so I was allowed to appear in more or less modern garb, to my great satisfaction and relief. I hadn't been looking forward to being critcally viewed by my extended Northern family in my medieval gear!

I have great memories of many American and European trips with Tom and Matt, after the second record came out. In those days, in the early 1970s, I was still playing both accordion and uilleann pipes, which meant that poor Tom, who only needed a whistle or flute for his own music, was usually saddled with the job of carrying my accordion half-way across the world. He used to joke about one of his arms being longer than the other from it all! We had been playing for the Irish Arts Center in New York some time previously, providing music for a play directed by film-star

Janice Roule, probably better known then as the wife of another star, Ben Gazzara. Brian Herron, grandson of the patriot James Connolly, had called her in to pull a fairly loosely constructed and self-indulgent play into shape, and Janice was just the woman for that job. Some of the stars were demoted in the process, and *Na Filí* given a more important role by her than had been envisaged for us. She left the actors bruised and muttering darkly of revolt. Connemara singer Seosamh O h-Eanaí was involved as well. For me, striking up a friendship with Joe Heaney, as he was known in America, a long-time hero of mine, made the American trip memorable. We both saw the humour in Janice Roule's upturning of the whole affair, to make music the winner. Janice was justified when the critics gave the show a good press and she moved up in the pecking order of the Arts Center.

America was a whole new experience and gave us many memories, like the time we were all seated on the floor in a smoke-filled room, the night after our first American concert. An American student rolled another cigarette and offered it to my friend Tom Barry, sitting on my left. 'Ah-h ... w-what is it?' Tom asked nervously. 'Grass, man – grass,' came the drawled answer. 'No, thank you very much,' said Tom, refusing the offer. The American looked at him patronisingly, as he might look at a child. And, in a way, we were children – at least in the context of America, music and drugs. We had just experienced a great reaction at our first concert in New York, meeting people whom we didn't know, but who knew us through our first two records.

I think it was on that visit that we were invited to march with the Arts Center group in the St Patrick's Day parade. It was the first Fifth Avenue parade since Derry's Bloody Sunday and the atmosphere was still tense, the authorities worried that the event might be used for publicity stunts. We had to wait a long time in a side-street off Fifth Avenue for our turn to step out boldly and join the rest of the marchers. As we waited, I saw a group with something I couldn't recognise, like flat wooden planks painted black. They were keeping their contraption well hidden from the stewards and police, who were everywhere. When we got the signal to go, we all surged forward. 'Up lads, now', a voice said, and they hoisted the object on to their shoulders, opening it out as they did so, to form a black coffin which they clearly meant to carry in the procession. I have never seen a reaction so swift as that of the stewards and police. In ten seconds they were bustling in among us. Up in the air went the coffin and down it crashed in a dozen useless pieces all around us. In a further ten seconds – no more – the wreckers were gone and our group took its place in the procession. No one else seemed to have noticed the protest – certainly not the Fifth Avenue crowds. There were no recriminations on either side and it had all happened so suddenly I began to wonder if it was real. But it was.

A month later, back in Ireland, I had to wonder about reality again, when I answered our telephone at five o'clock one very cold April morning. It was Janice Roule telling me that we just had to, repeat *had* to, come out again to New York the following night to play at a big party in Ben Gazzara's luxury apartment, a fundraiser for the Arts Center. It seemed they had just got confirmation of the proposed attendance of a number of important political figures, including Ted Kennedy and Bella, a leading socialite and fundraiser, whose surname I forget, though I do remember she was given to wearing enormous floral hats. That guaranteed the financial success of the evening, with big subscriptions from the best people in New York. It meant, too, that they could afford to fly *Na Filí* out and pay our expenses, though there was no fee involved. As I shivered in our cold hall that morning, I told her she was mad if she thought that we could just down tools and hop out to America to play for half an hour at a Ben Gazzara party. She said she'd ring back in six hours for my answer. I told her she could, if she wished, but that there wasn't really much point ...

Tom, Matt and myself laughed about it later that day: the thing was crazy and anyway, we were due to play at a concert in Clonakilty in two days. The more we talked about the craziness of it all, the nearer we drifted towards saying 'yes'. When Janice rang, that's exactly what I did say and the show was on the road. Aer Lingus phoned to say they had tickets waiting and we were bundled on to the plane, with our instruments and very little else. We circled Kennedy airport for about half an hour, with the three of us getting progressively more and more nervous, for we were due to start playing down there in a matter of minutes. If the pilot hadn't got us down quickly then, he might as well have turned round and brought us back to Shannon, for the New York show would have been over without us. Tom King was waiting, with the car engine running, to whizz us to the apartment, overlooking Central Park. I don't remember all the people we were introduced to, nor have I any clear memory of what we played, though everybody seemed happy and told us how wonderful we were!

I think we got some sleep before we took the plane back to Ireland, to find ourselves in a hall in Clonakilty, where Seán Ó Sé was announcing: '... And now, all the way from America, just to play for you tonight in Clonakilty – *Na Filí*.' Well, at least it was a true bill!

When we made our first appearance at the famous Loughborough Festival in England, we got enthusiastic reviews from the two big folk magazines of the time, *Melody Maker* and *New Musical Express*. According to *Melody Maker*: '*Na Filí* made an immense impression', while Eric Winter's Festival Report in *New Musical Express* talked about the group's marvellous reception and opined that *Na Filí* next year could name their own dates. In the New Year Awards of *New Musical Express* in the following year, *Na Filí* were awarded Best Instrumental Group prize. Those were wonderful years.

We had begun our European trips by the time our third record, *Na Filí 3*, appeared and we topped the bill at the Osnabruck Festival in Germany and attended the Nyon Festival a few times. *Planxty* were newcomers on the scene at this time and we had a pleasant day with them when we met at the Lenzburg Festival in Switzerland. It was an excellent event and I have very warm memories of listening to great music from piper Liam O'Flynn at a workshop there.

All our playing was done that day in Lenzburg Castle on a beautifully hot Sunday afternoon.

At this time, in the early 1970s, Fachtna O'Kelly wrote in an overall review of traditional music that:

> ... the only really innovative music coming out of the country is in the traditional field.
>
> Long gone are the days when the real Irish music was heard only in the rural areas of the country and the stage-Irishisms of Charlie McGee and his *Homes of Donegal* ruled the roost.
>
> In their place are the glorious sounds of bands like the *Chieftains*, *Na Filí* and *Planxty*, all retaining the basic traditional feel but developing on it until they can no longer be ignored by any self-respecting music lover of the seventies.
>
> When somebody finally gets around, in the years to come, to writing a full history of traditional Irish music, they might well decide the heady days of the seventies were the most exciting of all. With bands like the *Chieftains*, *Na Filí* and *Planxty* around, who could blame them?

We were, I would think, getting too much praise, so the begrudgers stepped in to redress the balance. Our fourth record, *A Kindly Welcome*, brought out by Dolphin, was rubbished by Mícheál Ó Domhnaill on *The Long Note* radio programme on RTE, mostly on the basis of a faulty pressing he had received. The producer of the programme, Tony McMahon wrote to me about it sometime later, in what seemed an attempt to excuse the programme's unethical performance. It was never obvious to me at the time whether the blatant bias of *The Long Note* was due to the presenter himself or to his producer. People in RTE were of the opinion that it had more to do with an attempt to shoot down the opposition before the launch of a new group. Whatever the reason, it represented a new bitterness that had not previously contaminated relationships among the three main Irish music groups, the *Chieftains*, *Na Filí* and *Planxty*, who had a high regard for each other. Irish music was starting a new journey into hype and commercialism.

After this the groups proliferated. *The Bothy Band* produced an exciting, very fast sound that caught the fancy of a younger set and they became a model for many learners. For me, their star was Paddy Keenan, who piped beautifully. I still remember being bowled over by his playing on a

89

record of an earlier group he played with and it prompted me to interview him for a book I was writing at the time, *Traditional Music in Ireland*. I remember meeting the group *Dé Danann* in Holland, I think, after we gave a concert there in the mid-1970s, but dates get confused at this distance from the event. In the second half of the 1970s we played a number of enjoyable concerts in Italy and were pleased to meet *Clannad*, who were always very musical, though not then so famous as they later became. Such meetings were always welcome, but occurred less frequently than you would expect, since each group tended to top the bill in its own concert. It was a different matter at big festivals, where many top groups were involved and things were more relaxed.

I used to have fairly constant ribbing about pipes from Matt and Tom. It was always good-natured and even sometimes helped in our stage presentation. I was the one who did the main talking to the audience about our programme, with various off-mike comments by my colleagues. One comment in particular stands out in my mind. We had been asked to play for the Galway mass for the Pope's visit and it turned out to be an exciting and inspiring occasion. When it was over, the Pope walked around the enormous stage, looking out at his audience. We were right up at the stage as he passed. In my enthusiasm, I held up the pipes and he looked down, smiled and made the sign of the cross in the air, in my direction. 'Look,' I said to Tom and Matt, 'he blessed my pipes.' My colleagues were not as impressed as I was: 'It would take more than a papal blessing to make that thing sound good,' they agreed. Clearly, I was not destined to become big-headed about my piping!

Things were becoming a bit hectic for us, between trying to maintain our normal jobs and yet giving a worthwhile amount of time to the group. A big London record company, Transatlantic, had signed us up to do a new LP and were keen that we should have a manager. I think it was they who recommended the London-based Ann Dex Agency to us, as she managed a number of other artists on their list. We went over to a studio in Worthing for a week, bringing our families with us and spent more time on one recording than we had ever done. It was quite pleasant to find out how the full-timers worked! Topping the bill at the Albert Hall Folk Prom was an unforgettable experience and we appeared many times at the Sidmouth Festival. It was around this time that we went to Cyprus on a concert tour with some of Ann Dex's other artists, including Jasper Carrot. My main memory of it all is how hot the Mediterranean was, with no shock to the system when you dipped a foot in it. That too was new!

The latest Transatlantic record, *The Chanter's Tune*, turned out well – we thought it the best we had ever done, both in terms of material and of sound-quality. I was particularly satisfied with the beautiful integration of voice and instruments, something I have always thought *Na Filí* did better than anyone. However, the record didn't really get a proper distribution, as, after more than a decade of playing across Europe and America, we finally decided to call it a day in 1979. We sent out a letter to organisers and papers letting them know that it was over. We had to resist many attempts since then to get us to change our minds, but we were determined not to follow the path of certain well-known groups of those days, who had a whole series of farewell concerts and then final farewell concerts, eventually reaching the farce of final, final farewells!

For myself, looking back on it all, I found the first half of the 1970s marvellous. I suppose we had a certain innocence then, a kind of wonder at a whole phenomenon that was still new and fresh. We were travelling largely untrodden paths that allowed us to be, to some extent at least, satisfyingly creative. The co-operation with Matt and Tom in musical matters I found inspiring and I learned a lot from them. No doubt I contributed to the sum total of our musical achievements in my own way. That way was probably concerned with singing and the playing of airs, though I have to say that all three of us had an instinctive feeling for the essence of the airs. Matt and Tom always had more to offer than I had in the dance music sphere, but I hope I was a reasonable learner there too. In fact, now that I think of it, learning is the number one skill of my life and the common denominator of my various endeavours!

MEET THE RUC

It is a pleasure to acknowledge my indebtedness to Francey McPeake, for his encouragement and for his practical piping help in the 1960s. I remember the unusual style that Francey himself and his father had acquired. Old Francey had been taught by a well-known blind piper, O'Reilly from Galway and was mentioned by the collector, Francis O'Neill, for winning the junior piping competition in Dublin at the 1912 Oireachtas and for singing to his own piping, a feature of the McPeake family style since. The Northern piper and pipe-maker, O'Mealy, also influenced the old man's piping and their intricate method of decorating a tune, called by the Americans, 'backstitching', is something I learned from Francey. It is a pleasure to acknowledge that, particularly since neither of the two Franceys that I am discussing are with us any longer.

I was still making occasional visits to Francey McPeake, after old Francey died. One such trip to Belfast, to have a piping session with Francey in 1968, led to a confrontation with the RUC, a court case and even my imprisonment for a time. Let me explain.

I was looking forward to a session with Francey McPeake that Sunday afternoon. I was in Belfast visiting my mother and had brought a practice-set of pipes with me from Cork. The sun was shining and I decided to walk across from the Antrim Road and turn up the Falls. I had only gone a few yards up, when I saw a ball coming out on to the road from a square on the left, where there was a group playing football. A young lad ran out to retrieve the ball and at that very moment an RUC motorcyclist drove up the Falls, stopped and held the young fellow. I still had not reached the place where all this was happening so quickly, but I could see it plainly in front of me. Just then, an RUC car drove up and stopped. The RUC motorcyclist spoke to them, still holding the young fellow. The car drove off, turning right up a side-road.

The motorcyclist, to my surprise, then got the young fellow in an arm-lock, as I heard the high-pitched sound of a car reversing at speed. It was the police car coming out of the side-street and stopping beside the motorcyclist. One of the policemen jumped out, opened the back door and pushed the young lad inside. With that, a man ran across the road from the square where the game had been played and began to remonstrate with the police. I assumed it was probably the lad's father and later confirmed that it was. Some other people had come from the square and were gathering near the police-car. I went over and spoke to the driver, asking where they were taking the two people they had in the car. 'Hastings Street', was the answer – something which I later had cause to know was not true. I told him I would like to give an independent view of the events as I had seen them. The car was about to drive off and as it did, a lady hit the top of the boot with her hand, saying something which I didn't hear, but which I gathered was not very complimentary to the RUC. Nowadays, of course, the RUC would not even notice such a trivial incident, but those were other days and the RUC were not used to such summary treatment by anyone from the Falls. They were not prepared to accept it in this case.

The car stopped immediately and the policeman in the passenger's seat came out, looking angrily at the crowd. 'Who did that?' he asked. The motorcycle policeman pointed to a man at the back of the crowd, saying: 'That's him.' With that, the policeman who had asked the question walked away in the direction of a man who was yards away from the car and couldn't possibly have thumped it. I was shocked and got into conversation with the driver, pointing out that everything seemed to me to have been started by the RUC motorcyclist. The driver was a very pleasant man, who had no problem talking to me, though, of course, he didn't agree with my analysis of events.

The other policeman came striding back, grabbed me by the arm, saying, 'we're having you for obstruction', pushed me into the back of the car with the others and drove away. I was surprised, of course, at my new condition, but satisfied that I would be getting an opportunity to tell what had really happened. We didn't go to Hastings Street, but to another centre-city barrack, whose name I have forgotten. We were escorted inside to a desk, where my name, address and occupation were noted, as were the details of the others. I was amazed to be charged with obstruction and even more put-out when I was locked into a cell for the first time in my life.

After some time, perhaps half-an-hour, the motorcycle policeman came to the grill in the door of the cell, looked in and said: 'I'm having you for a disturbance of the peace, as well.' After all this time – it happened in 1968 – I cannot be completely sure of his exact words and I did not know the law well enough to know whether the charge needed some form of assent from me. I decided to say nothing, but just stared at him and he went away.

Eventually, the sergeant looked in and asked if I wanted to call home, as I could be given bail, pending my appearance in court next morning. I knew I certainly couldn't ring my mother, as she would be distraught at the thought of her respectable son being held by the RUC, so I tried to contact James McPeake, who was a taximan at the time, working from a centre-city depot. He wasn't there, but a colleague of his, whom I knew, offered to come over and see if he could help. He was told that he could bail me out for £25 – no small sum in those days. As it happened, I had a cheque-book in my pocket, with one last cheque in it, which I made out to him for £25, just in case anything went wrong and he had to pay the bail. The sergeant was very kind and recommended that I get in touch with a solicitor before the next day's hearing.

The only solicitor I knew at the time was Séamus Napier, whom I contacted. He told me he would not be available as he would be out of town, but he put me in touch with his brother, Oliver Napier, who was to become well-known years later as the leader of the Alliance party in the North. I went to court next day, to be told by my solicitor that he would try to get a postponement of the case, since, in his opinion, I had no chance of getting a judgement against the RUC from the particular judge whose court we were in that day.

In court, Oliver said that, due to my position as a University lecturer, it was vital for me to have time to prepare my case properly and on the basis of his plea, he was granted a deferral of at least some weeks, perhaps even a month. This also applied to the case against the man from the Falls and his son.

I was interviewed by newspaper reporters afterwards, so I knew I had better be in touch with University College Cork, just to let them know that I hadn't suddenly lost the run of myself, no matter what the newspapers might say next day! I was in touch with Helen in Cork. She told me later that she had been talking to Séamus Caomhánach, who was deputy President of UCC at the time. She must have said something about being worried about the University's attitude and Séamus said to her: 'Some of Tomás' colleagues, far from being worried if they were in his situation, would be looking for a medal!' I had a good defender in a research student of mine at the time, Joe King, who gave a good telling-off to a member of staff in Cork who suggested, when he saw it reported in a newspaper, that I would have been much better-off minding my own business in Belfast, rather than getting mixed up in things that didn't concern me.

I didn't expect that the court case would worry me very much, but it did. I think this had more to do with the long wait for the case to be called again. I found myself a bit edgy with people, even with my mother the day before the second court appearance, when I felt it necessary to explain to her that I was worried about going into court to hear the RUC tell lies about the events of that Sunday on the Falls, and the almost inevitable result, in those pre-1969 days, that I would be found guilty of something I had not done. Worst of all was that I thought I had never done anything in my life with less self-interest involved. I was surprised recently when my cousin, Harry Coyle, in Derry told me that he remembered me saying in those days that I would mortgage the house over my head, if necessary, to see justice done. I'm glad my wife Helen wasn't in on that particular conversation!

Oliver Napier decided that for the second hearing he would involve QC Turlough O'Donnell, who was a barrister of high standing in the Northern courts and would, within a few years, become Chief Justice. Having a QC to defend me was intended to show the court how seriously we regarded the whole business. Also there was the man from the Falls, with his solicitor. The RUC were first to put their case: I was more than a little annoyed as I listened to them, continually implying that, while my intentions might not have been bad, I was just a well-meaning do-gooder who did not help in the situation. I consoled myself by realising that I would have my own opportunity, when I was called, to tell the true story of all that had happened. Turlough O'Donnell cross-questioned the police and made some valuable points. Then, to my utter horror, he said he was not calling me! I wrote a quick note and passed it up to Oliver Napier, who was sitting beside the Falls man's solicitor. 'He must call me,' I said. Oliver shook his head, but the other solicitor answered my note with another: 'I'll call you', was all it said. I had forgotten that I was probably his star witness.

Just then, the judge asked both sides to come to his room for a discussion. I am ashamed to say that I was a bit unhappy about it, wondering what sort of plot the two legal teams and the judge were hatching while the rest of us waited. I am sure my Catholic experience of the RUC and the whole legal system was to blame for my nasty suspicions, which were, in fact, completely unfounded. When the court resumed, the judge announced that he was dismissing all charges against me. What a relief! It was only later I heard that he had asked the RUC to withdraw their charges, but they refused, no doubt feeling that they might make themselves liable to a different kind of legal battle.

In the packed court were all our family, including my mother. Also there was my friend, the late Francey

McPeake, to whom I had been going for a piping session on the fateful Sunday. I know Francey was keen to have me win, not only for my own sake, but, in a curious way, to make up for what he saw as the many injustices his people had suffered in the past at the hands of the RUC. I was to be the means to that end. He was sitting beside my mother and sisters and it was obvious to them that he was overjoyed at the judge's statement.

The case then began against the man from the Falls, with his solicitor cross-questioning the police. I was called eventually and asked to describe what had happened, which I did, in answer to various questions. Among other things, I described how the motorcycle policeman had got the young lad in an arm-lock. The judge then intervened, saying: 'Are you aware that it is possible to get a completely wrong impression of a situation when you come on it suddenly?' I said I was. He then said: 'I want you to think carefully before you answer my next question: are you sure the policeman had the young fellow in an arm-lock?' I paused to let him see that I was taking his instruction about careful thought to heart.

Unknown to me, though I heard about it afterwards, Francey McPeake, sitting beside my mother, got very worried at my silence. No doubt, he could suddenly see his hope of revenge for the past disappearing. My mother heard him exhorting me, under his breath: 'You saw him, Tom: say you f....n' saw him!' He was relieved to hear me say that I had positively seen exactly what I had already described to the court. That seemed to be the turning-point. The judge announced that he was dismissing all charges against the Falls man as well.

A lady came to me outside the court, calling every blessing from God down on my head: she was the wife of the Falls man, who had been cleared on the basis of my evidence. It seems things would have been very bad for him otherwise, as he had a previous conviction. I remember being interviewed by some reporters after the case. One of them asked me an interesting question: 'If the same thing happened again as you walked up the Falls, would you do the same again, considering the trouble all this has caused you?' I told him that I didn't really know, but that I would be ashamed of myself if I didn't. That got a big heading in the next day's *Daily Express*. The billboard's for that evening's *Belfast Telegraph* carried the headline: 'University Don cleared of charges.' Walking down Royal Avenue after the case, I felt I owned Belfast, such was my elation and relief at the result. But all that was in the heyday of the RUC. Things would soon be changing.

Earlier in that summer of 1968, when things were really hotting up in the North, with the 'O'Neill Must Go' campaign strongly backed by Paisley and his supporters, Helen and I went down Sandy Row on Bonfire night, which, in the North, means the night before the twelfth of July. The atmosphere was electric, with enormous fires at each end, that were being fed with old furniture and anything that would blaze. As heavy items were thrown on, they were accompanied by what were obviously sincere and forceful wishes concerning the Pope – and not for the poor man's good! Things were already more than a little sectarian when a van drove up and people began to sell Ian Paisley's paper – I think it was called *The Protestant Telegraph* – which at that time was serialising a violently anti-Catholic story entitled, 'The Jesuit'.

The following day, I took a cine-camera with me and followed the Orange parade to 'The Field', hoping to get some good pictures. There was one cordoned-off section where speeches were being made. I went over and stood outside it, at the wire netting, listening to fairly provocative outpourings. One was given by Mr Kirk, minister of Education, as far as I can remember, in Terence O'Neill's government. His supporters would clap him pretty frequently, while others shouted: 'O'Neill Must Go'. As I was in a fairly conspicuous situation and couldn't bring myself to clap what I was hearing, I would put the cine up to my eye and pretend to be taking a picture at every clapping time. I must have been noticed. A man behind me shouted: 'We shouldn't be fightin' among ourselves: it's them Fenians is the trouble.' With that, he put two arms around me from behind and held on to the wire fence, imprisoning me between himself and it, so that I couldn't move. 'You're not one of them, are you?' he shouted into my ear.

There is a time in everyone's life when they should stand up and be counted, when they should be prepared to acknowledge what they believe in. Clearly this was my moment. Thoughts of my ancestors and of the faith of our forefathers and other such noble concepts circled inside my head. In a slightly hoarse voice that could not have been too convincing, I made it crystal-clear where I stood. 'No', I croaked, and he released me. I didn't hang around too long after that!

POETRY FOR LIFE

I wouldn't call myself a poet, though I have written many verses in my time. I can't look back to a particular moment when my interest in poetry was initiated, for it was always there and life without it is unimaginable. I haven't tried to write about these things before, but I feel that an interest in poetry is almost as natural as breathing and needs no explanation or justification. This has nothing to do with an ability to write poetry, since I am strongly of the opinion that being a poet has more to do with a mental approach to life than with a facility in stringing words together.

It was in St Columb's College in Derry that I first came in contact with any sort of analysis of poetry. Our English teacher was Mr Frank McAuley, who seemed to us a real writer, since he wrote regularly for the local paper, the *Derry Journal*. He was a firm believer in pre-programming us for public examinations, by laboriously dictating notes on the poets and their poetry, which we had to write down and learn off by heart. I always had a good memory, as had many of my classmates in St Columb's. Even yet, when I meet Seán McMahon or Réamonn Ó Gallchóir, former classmates, a single word can unleash a duet of Frank McAuley's poetry notes. As an example, if the name Flecker is mentioned we go into free-flight with: 'James Elroy Flecker was one of the most promising modern English poets, had he not died so young. He served in the British Consular service at Smyrna ...' and so on until we run out of words. There was another English teacher in the school who scorned this method and had what was probably a more literary approach to poetry. In defence of Frank McAuley, I must say his method concentrated one's attention on the poet. His rather arbitrary marking of individual verses of the poems to be learned by us and recited next day in class, had its detractors, but he turned out generations of students who had a built-in standard of reference for the rest of their lives. Hundreds, probably many thousands of us, are testimony to that. Frank McAuley's system was a good one in the narrow field of preparation for public examinations and a proven success there, but it was much more – it was his monument and a worthwhile one.

My first few poems, which were in Irish, did not become written words until I was 30. The first was in response to our new and marvellous child Nuala, when she started to crawl, and I, like every father before me, had a vision of how wonderful the moment was and yet could realise that these were the first steps away from us and into her own future, with our blessing. The second was a reaction to the first big famine in Ethiopia and to the awfulness of a disaster that drove every good thought from the mind, except the blinding pain of hunger:

OCRAS

Aoibh an gháire
Na caint chliste
Ní bhíonn ann
In aimsir ghorta;
Ach pian an ocrais
Ag dalladh na h-intinne.

Pleasure of laughter
Or clever chatter
Are not found
In famine time;
Only hunger's pain
That blinds the mind.

Craiceann righin
Ar chnámha teannta
Cíocha seasca
Nach dtál deor;
Deireadh a shaoil
Ag leanbh scréachach.

Taut skin
Stretched over bone
Barren breasts
With nothing to give;
The end of life
For a screaming child.

Ni chaointear na mairbh,
Mar ní h-ábhar caointe
Scaoileadh an ghlais
Ag an ocras fáiscithe
Ar intinn aibí
Go mbí sí millte.

Dead are not keened,
No cause for keening
Breaking of the bond
That hunger tightens
On the quick mind
Until it cease.

Ní h-ábhar caointe
An fhuiseog mhear
Ag díriú léi
I dtreo na gréine
Agus ceol na saoirse
Aici dá chanadh.

No cause for keening
The swift lark
That points itself
Towards the sun
Singing the music
Of freedom.

Is a Dhia Mhór	Great God
An ag magadh bhí tú	Were you joking
An t-am ar thoilís	When you ordained
An bolg ataithe	The swollen belly
Ina lorg ocrais	To be hunger's stigma
Ar chorpán cloíte?	On the wasted corpse?
Bocht an luach	What a miserable bargain
Builín aráin	A loaf of bread
Ar bheatha duine	For a life
Ab fhiú, uair,	Once worth
Céasadh is crochadh	Crucifixion
Is coróin spíne.	And a crown of thorns.

I was fortunate to be a friend of Bríd and Pat Crotty when I took my first steps in what I might call real poetry, whatever that is. By *real poetry* I mean poetry that the average reader would be attracted to, as much for its language as for its message – I do not mean the literary posing and pirouetting that often passes as poetry in the self-sustaining circle of scribblers who have nothing to say, but say it so beautifully! Bríd and Pat were both teachers in Cork, before they took up jobs in Wales, and Pat was subsequently Editor of *Modern Irish Poetry: An Anthology*. Pat Crotty was a good judge of the rightness of lines or phrases and had an instinctive and sure touch in pointing out the weak parts of a poetic structure. More than anything else, I learned from him the importance of working on the lines until they became a more efficient vehicle for the thought. Pat probably wouldn't say it that way, but that is how I interpret his approach. He would never try to re-write a poem, but would leave you with a pretty clear idea of where work could be done on it. I didn't always agree with him at first, but I usually found, when I had done the required work, that he had been right again.

Pat's wife Bríd was of great assistance to me when I was writing the autobiographical novel, *Home to Derry* which was published some years ago. Her touch in assessing prose was just as sure as her husband's was in poetry. I would often drop in to their house in Hackett's Terrace on my way home from Dublin. That Cork-Dublin train never failed to inspire me to write some sort of poetry, as long as I could avoid meeting friendly human beings who wanted to talk! The man who put them in the class of 'Enemies of Promise' was not far wrong. The plane to London was once kind and gave me a poem, as we circled the city for ages, waiting for permission to land. Each time we banked and turned, the Thames rose up on its side and showed me a poem, which I captured straightaway. In those days I would judge public transport by its generosity with poems. But, as they say in Irish: d'imigh sin agus tháinig seo – that went and this came. To remember those days of travelling by train to meetings of the Cultural relations Committee of the Department of Foreign Affairs, here is a poem that happened one evening on the return journey:

TRAINSCAPE

At Mallow, the Blackwater gathers to itself
The rushy fields of squelching cattle
That have followed us from Charleville,
And trout-swollen streams in white-rimmed
Fields, whose virginal thorn is shocked
By vibrant tingle of saffron gorse.

In the air, a darting team of synchronised
Swallows wheel, stall, change gear,
Dive low, where a pair of thoroughbreds,
Grazing in a rushless field, start-up
To race the passing train for sport.

Careless cows graze where they can,
In a multi-coloured haggard of crashed cars;
TV aerials scrape the sky
For snowy signals from greener fields.

Unmoved, in the rath's dark circle,
Old trees murmur in council.

I find that poetry lets me speak about things I should address and yet do not, for all sorts of reasons, which are generally involved with my own background and its accepted conventions. When I write prose, I am mostly dealing with facts or perhaps with opinions directly related to them, but poetry asks me to go deeper into myself. Without wishing to be too precious about it, I see poetry as being on a higher plane than ordinary language and going deeper than the surface treatment ordinary writing gives its subjects. It is a common experience of anyone who writes, that the written word takes over and establishes a momentum and an energy that are somehow independent of the writer. That certainly happens to me and the result is often a surprise and a new realisation of my own true feelings, until then unexpressed. I would certainly go along with those who would regard the writing of poetry as being an exploration of oneself. No doubt, it is therapeutic in some sense, but those writers, and there are some in poetry clubs who write poetry as a substitute for a visit to a therapist, are missing the point – which is writing poetry for poetry's sake. Only then will you find the golden key that opens the inner doors.

I met quite a few recognised poets at the Poetry International in Rotterdam in 1973, when I was asked to go as piper with the Irish delegation, as there was to be an emphasis on Celtic poetry that year. Hugh mac Diarmaid was there from Scotland and Alan Ginsberg from America. Robert Lowell was the other famous American there. The Irish group included John Montague and Mícheál Ó h-Uanacháin, with myself on pipes. We co-operated loosely with the Scottish and Friesland groups in a Celtic workshop. Helen and I became very friendly with the Swedish poet Ivan Malinovski and his wife Ruth, who subsequently visited us in Ireland and stayed a few days in Cork. Over the years, Ivan would send us various poetry books of his as they were published, but there won't be any more, as Ivan died a few years ago. We were sorry to get the bad news from Ruth that the big gentle poet had gone. He was one of the small number of 'real' people in Rotterdam that year – so many of the others were walking characterisations of themselves!

Günter Grass gave a lecture that we all attended and few of us understood and there was a performance of one of his plays in an ultra-modern setting in a huge theatre called Die Dolin, where most of the functions of the festival took place. My other low-grade memory of the Rotterdam

Poetry International is of a huge Indonesian dinner, given for us all in a city-centre restaurant, with something like 20 different courses. Culture was well-served in Rotterdam, but the food was good too, let it be said!

I had another small fling with poetry in the Irish language a few years ago, when I attended the Court of Poetry, or Cúirt Filíochta that is held at the beginning of each year in Cúil Aodha, Co. Cork. Since it is set in the heart of Muskerry, it is called in Irish, *Damh-Scoil Mhúscraí*. Each year a different theme is set and the poets must respond to it poetically, in front of a knowledgeable audience, many of whom have been attending here, every January for a lifetime.

Helen and I set up a small publishing company in 1987 to publish occasional poetry books. My first collection of poetry was called *Melos*, which seemed suitable, since *Melos* is the Greek root for the word melody. Gerald Goldberg launched it in the Collins Bookshop in Careys Lane, Cork and it sold out fairly quickly. I tried to combine, in this collection, what I would call family poetry, with poems on music and even with a sideways glance at the North, as I saw it from the South. Some of the poems weren't bad, but others had begun to veer towards the style of the scribblers I spoke about before, who had nothing much to say, but said it so beautifully. I started to think about some earlier poems from what I might call my 'peasant' period, in the days when the message itself was really all I wanted to get right. Such poems I had not included in *Melos*, which aimed a little higher, I thought. I remember one of those poems, about my grandfather – not the one I have quoted elsewhere, but a simpler one that maybe says just as much:

FRANCEY

Your music has gone Francey, out of Carnanban,
Though the fields still crop and the trees grow
And it's little you'd think now there was a time
When they crowded in to hear your fiddle sing.

But that fine song is long since sung
And Patrick, your son, who sang it too
Is taken away and his fiddle's gone
And the crows caw in Carnanban.

High grow those trees that were young with you
And have watched these three generations go:
Christ, is it right that a tree can stay
When Francey and his music are blown away?

But no tree will best you, Francey Murphy,
For the seed of your song is blown in my mouth
And you'll lack neither voice nor my fingers' span
To flower an echo in Carnanban.

SEÁN Ó RIADA

The first time I met Seán Ó Riada I had the nerve to tell him that he had been singing out of tune on a television programme of his, which had been broadcast some time previously. It was 1963 and Seán had just joined the staff of UCC. I was introduced to him with some others at a big College function in the student restaurant, where we all stood around talking. But Seán soon corrected me about his singing, pointing out that he had been in tune alright, even though it might not have sounded great, as he didn't claim to be a singer. That wasn't the most auspicious start to a friendship I cherished for the next eight years, with a man who could be both rough and gentle, both cocksure and quite unsure, but always fascinating – the only genius I've ever met.

I remember our family going to visit Sean in Coolea once for Sunday afternoon tea. It was our first visit and Seán had suggested I bring my accordion for a session. One of the tunes we played was a Northern version of the Donegal reel, with Seán on fiddle. Nothing wonderful about that, you might say, but Seán's strong anti-accordion views were well-known after his radio series, *Our Musical Heritage*. When I took him to task about those views he laughed and said: 'You sometimes have to exaggerate to make a point.' It was a technique of argument he often used. He believed in overkill – the finer details could be filled in later, when the opponent had already been completely vanquished!

He was very proud of his first mass and sent some of us the Ár nAthair (Our Father) from it as a Christmas card in his own elegant hand. Later on he showed me the cover of that Coolea mass-book just before it was published, pointing out details of the excellent design. He always knew he was doing something a bit special with the Coolea choir, which had started from sessions held in his house, at which the local seanchaí, Tadhg Ó Maoláin presided. Seán suggested to An tAthair Donncha Ó Conchúir that the lads who sang in his house could, with some training, sing in the church. They decided to begin with Benediction and learned *O Salutaris Hostia, Tantum Ergo* and *Caoineadh na dTrí Muire*. Gradually their repertoire increased, with *Mo Ghrása mo Dhia* and a new *Ár nAthair* that Seán composed for them. He was fastidious about their learning the exact meaning of what they sang, giving rise to competition among themselves in providing nicely-turned native translations for the Benediction hymns. The music for this first mass was solidly based in local tradition and this is most clearly felt in his settings of *Rí an Domhnaigh* and *Gile mo Chroí*, this last piece set to the air of a traditional song collected from Murt Sé. But singing at mass did not meet with universal acceptance in Coolea, some of the parishioners feeling that this new Vatican Two nonsense of singing in the vernacular was taking things a bit too far. As well as that, it interfered with their rosaries!

In 1968 I decided to do the Bachelor of Music degree and we had Seán as our lecturer in Irish music, keyboard harmony and history. He was inspirational in Irish music, had the keenest musical ear imaginable in our keyboard class, but tended towards a surprising dogmatism in his musical history. For him, Mozart was marvellous, Beethoven bad, Bach beautiful and Handel horrible. An English extern examiner, who was an authority on George Frederick Handel, nearly had apoplexy when he read what some of Seán's students thought of his beloved composer!

Seán Ó Riada had become a member of staff in the Music Department after the retirement of Seán Neeson. Ó Riada lectured in both Irish Music and on the history of Western music. I found him an excellent and inspiring lecturer, though I know that opinion was not shared by everyone. Certainly, our class always enjoyed very good relations with him and we looked forward to his classes. I know from later discussion with Professor Fleischmann that such had not always been the case and that there had been complaints in earlier years about his attendance and commitment to the course – so much so that there had been a major confrontation between him and Professor Fleischmann, when Seán threatened to resign.

Seán was our instructor in keyboard skills, when each of us in turn performed modulations at the piano, on his instructions. We were all deeply impressed by the keenness of his musical ear: no matter how many notes you would put into a chord, Seán could, at a distance, tell you immediately what note was unacceptable and which finger was playing it! The main trick in keyboard work was to avoid consecutive fifths and octaves in your progressions. I soon discovered a fairly fool-proof way of doing that, which served me well in examinations, but which did nothing for my musical education. Another part of the test was to recognise chords and their inversions when Seán played them on piano. This was made a little easier by the fact that we always felt he was on our side at the official aural test.

Seán had a considerable interest in technical things, especially if they were a bit gimmicky. I remember being involved at the time with transistor circuits for electronic metronomes – little devices that clicked out the required tempo of a piece of music – long before they had become common items in the stock of music shops. I had manufactured one that fitted inside a matchbox, with its own battery and speaker, which I showed to Seán. Nothing would satisfy him but to have one in his pocket, so I gave him mine and made another.

During this period, I was, of course, lecturing and researching full-time in Electical Engineering. Our professor in the Department, Charlie Dillon, was always very supportive of my other activities, which did not, in fact, impinge on my engineering commitments, as the Music Department had scheduled their lectures for late evening or Saturday morning, to suit the many teachers whom Professor Fleischmann had attracted to the B. Mus course. But some engineering students, particularly those in the Choral Society who would be meeting music students on a regular basis, thought it a bit unusual.

I worked hard in that first year, doing piano with Bridget Doolan in the Cork School of Music, organ in St

Finbarre's Cathedral with John T. Horne and making sure that no gaps were left in my defence. In the oral examination we were obliged to play Irish dance music on whistle, as part of the Irish Music examination – I think it earned a possible 15% of the marks in that paper. I played pipes, which got Sean's approval, and he was very complimentary afterwards, it being the first time he had heard me playing them, for I had been an accordionist in some earlier musical sessions with him in Coolea.

I could probably have got permission to play the pipes as my main instrument for the B. Mus, even though that had not been done before, but I saw it as more of a challenge to be like everyone else and play Bach, Beethoven, Mozart, Debussy and Chopin on piano. I was lucky in my piano-teacher, of course. I remember saying to a colleague in those days that Bridget Doolan could teach good piano to anyone who had a pair of hands and a backside to sit upon. I didn't mean that to be relayed to her, but it was: and she took it as a compliment, which it certainly was.

I was surprised to find that I had done very well at the First Year examination. History now shows that I stopped my intensive work then and failed to live up to my early promise. In second and third year, Bridget was very dispointed with my lack of practice and suggested, rather sarcastically, that I should play, as my main instrument, one which I had only recently taken-up – the cello. Equally, Professor Fleischmann began to complain that I was not submitting enough harmony and counterpoint homework. One of my classmates, Mary O'Callaghan, christened me Dr Doolittle, imitating the Professor's formal address of 'Dr Ó Canainn'. It was only years later, long after I had joined his staff as a lecturer, that Aloys unbent sufficiently to call me Tomás. Mind you, he did enjoy Mary O'Callaghan's appropriate name for me.

For me, one of the most enjoyable parts of the degree course was orchestral conducting. We were obliged to score a work for each year of the B. Mus course and conduct the piece, played by the Cork Symphony Orchestra. It was strings only in first year, strings and woodwind for second

111

year and full orchestra for the B. Mus. After the first year, I wrote my own music for the orchestra, rather than scoring an existing work, as the majority of students did. Standing up in front of the full orchestra and making them do what you wanted was a daunting, though exciting, task. It put all kinds of mad musical notions into my mind, but later events prevented some of my madnesses. I don't know if I regret that or not!

Our class saw another side of Seán Ó Riada when he was in dispute with Charles Acton, who had written in his review of one of Seán's concerts that the Corkman had used sentimental Mendelssohnian harmonies in his playing of Irish music on the piano. Seán was hurt by the comment and spoke to us about it in class. He played some of the music, asking us did we think the harmony was Mendelssohnian. Apart from the fact of whether it was or not, my feeling was one of sadness that Seán felt the need of reassurance from our class. I think we saw him as being far above that. He seemed much more vulnerable then, than I had ever seen him. Soon afterwards, *The Irish Times* correspondence between himself and Charles Acton began to appear, in which things were written that neither would have said if they could have known the events of the next few tragic months.

Being a colleague of Seán's, as well as his student, I could take some liberties with him, but he could too, as you shall hear. The book we used for history was Professor Meller's, *Man and his Music*, and we generally studied one chapter per class. I was intrigued, at one stage, to find that we were due to study three pre-Baroque German composers, with the unprepossessing names of Schutz, Schein and Scheidt. On my way into his lecture I let Seán know that I was looking forward to hearing how he was going to deal with these vulgar-sounding names in front of a class that included nuns and brothers. He just smiled and said: 'You'll see.' When he came into the class he looked straight down at me and said: 'Tomás wants to tell us about today's composers', so I was left with the dirty job of saying the bad words, much to everyone's amusement.

I brought my mother out to Coolea to meet him once. Seán was on the riverbank that day, looking happier than he had been for a long time, as he controlled his cast, to tempt a trout. My mother was a great admirer of his and was glad when he put away his fishing rod and we all went down to the Mills pub in Ballyvourney for a drink and a chat. Seán could be a real charmer and my mother thought he was a lovely man. She talked about her father Francey Murphy, who had been a fiddler and I let Seán know that she herself was a fiddler too, even though she usually tended to hide that fact in conversation. My mother spoke about that day for years and she always felt what I can only describe as a motherly care for Seán.

Our class visited him in the Bon Secours hospital that summer of 1971, not realising just how ill he really was. His mother came into the room and started fussing over pillows. Seán was almost apologising to us for her solicitude, kidding her at the same time and we had some good laughs with him that day. How could we have known then that there was so little time left for laughing?

Seán's sister, Louise Verling, got an urgent message that September from Fr James Good, telling her that he had visited her brother that day in the hospital and he was not at all well. In fact, An tAthair Donncha had given him the last rites of the Church. The Verlings had just returned from a holiday in their house in Connemara, but decided to come on directly to Cork to see Seán. They were shocked to find him so ill that they were not allowed in to visit him.

Next day there were high-level discussions in the hospital about what should be done. The family was advised to get another opinion and Garech de Brúin was instrumental in putting them in contact with a liver specialist in King's College Hospital, London. It was agreed that Seán should go there, but there was no available plane to take him. Garech was in touch with the chief of Aer Lingus and the result of their discussion was that an aeroplane was diverted to pick up Seán in Cork and bring him to London.

Seán Ó Sé went up to the airport on 14 September to see Ó Riada off and found that there was a problem. The owners of the private ambulance that had brought him from the hospital were not willing to let the stretcher be taken on to the aeroplane, in case they wouldn't get it back again, so Seán Ó Sé rang his friend, the singer John O'Shea, who arranged for one to be sent from the fire-station in which he worked. While they waited for it, a doctor from the hospital kept adjusting the drip into Ó Riada's arm, and as the two Seáns spoke, Seán Ó Sé got a sudden impression of his friend as a rabbit in a trap, looking up at his captors. When the stretcher was lifted into the plane, Seán Ó Sé said good-bye and mentioned the possibility of them seeing each other again soon, but Ó Riada indicated that he thought they might not. Before the patient was finally settled in his room in King's Hospital that day, there was a further stretcher problem, as the Cork stretcher was too big to fit into the hospital lift and Seán had to be taken up the fire-escape on the outside of the building. They had a long wait up there before the key of his room could be found.

Seán was operated-on in London and seemed to be progressing satisfactorily, until, after two heart-attacks, he died on Sunday 3 October. I had not known about it on that Sunday, until my neighbour, Séamus Ruiséal, who had just heard it on his car-radio, knocked at the window of our sitting-room, where *Na Filí* were practising. His words are still etched on my brain: 'Tá an Riadach caillte.' After that awful news we couldn't play another note. We had been under the impression that poor Seán was on the mend.

His remains came back to Cork airport on Tuesday 5 October and a tremendous crowd accompanied him to Coolea. Séamus Murphy, the famous Cork sculptor, asked me to give him a lift out to Coolea and provide some unskilled assistance in making Ó Riada's death-mask late that evening in the church. We were locked in there for some hours after the ceremonies that night, until the undertaker returned at an early hour of the morning to let us out, when the job was done. That was a memorable, if eerie, evening, as I had the very last view of poor Seán, God rest him. He had a magnificent funeral next day, with piper Alf Kennedy leading an enormous crowd from the church to the graveyard some miles away. That crowd included two people Seán Ó Riada would have been pleased to see there – Tom Barry, the west-Cork patriot and Charlie Haughey, the former Taoiseach. Seeing that funeral, no one could have doubted the national esteem in which Seán was held. John Kelly, the Clare fiddler who had been a member of Ceoltóirí Cualann and a particular friend of Ó Riada, said something that day that many others felt: 'He lifted us all up.'

PRESIDENTS AND PRECEDENTS

My adult life has always been what I would regard as double-sided! By that I mean that I have always had at least two strings to my bow – something I used to see as desirable. However, my University experience has gone a long way towards convincing me that, while they may make liberal noises in this regard, authorities in such institutions are not at all happy with the situation when it is presented to them in practice. They will always say 'yes' to the theory, but a firm 'no' to the practice. At least, that is what I found in my sometimes uncomfortable, though always enjoyable journey through one such institution.

To be fair, I think things have changed in the last ten years or so. Universities here have become more like their American counterparts, who have for a long time realised, to put it at its lowest level, that if you can get a couple of jobs out of an individual who is mad enough to do both for the one salary, then, all things being equal, you run with that situation. C.P. Snow and his two cultures were alright, as long as one didn't take such things too seriously: they were good subjects for graduation-day speeches, of course, but that was all.

Soon after I got the B. Mus in 1971 – in September, as far as I can remember – while Seán Ó Riada was seriously ill in King's College Hospital, London, Professor Fleischmann asked me if I would give the lectures in Irish Music in the Department for the first term, because it looked as if Seán would be in hospital for longer than we had thought. I was surprised, but told him I would, if Professor Charlie Dillon in the Electrical Engineering Department had no objection. Charlie was his usual obliging self and agreed to the new arrangement. However, within the month, Seán died and Aloys asked me to give the lectures for an indefinite period.

As their newly-appointed lecturer I felt sorry for the students, who would have expected to be listening to Seán talking about Irish Music. They were kind to me, as I tried to give them a view of Irish music and a look at the Indian tradition, both of which were inevitably coloured by Seán's views. My first B. Mus class included people like Mícheál Ó Súilleabháin, Eilís Cranitch, Nóirín Ní Riain, Máire Ní Bhuachalla and Seán Fitzpatrick, who has since directed the Cork Choral Festival.

The only significant change I can claim for my Irish Music teaching was the introduction of a compulsory project that obliged students to go out and collect living Irish music. For many of them, this brought their first visit to the gael-tacht to listen to and record real seán-nós singing, or per-haps, fiddling, and the chance to form their own opinions on the Irish tradition, rather than take their lecturer's view as gospel. This resulted in some pretty amateur recordings and sketchily-written reports initially, but formed a basis on which, with the assistance of the Audio-Visual Depart-ment in UCC, students of later years could begin a useful archive. I am glad to say that this archive was largely due to the work of Mícheál Ó Súilleabháin, who took over when I resigned after some four years.

They were four enjoyable years, as far as my connection with the Music Department and its students, under Professor Fleischmann, was concerned. However, after the first year, the President of the College, Dr M.D. McCarthy, began a series of pressure meetings with Professor Fleischmann to persuade him that I should not, as a Statutory Lecturer in Electrical Engineering, be giving the Irish Music lectures. This, notwithstanding the fact that it was he who had or-iginally approved the arrangement. The Professor told him that he wanted me to continue lecturing in the Music De-partment and I confirmed to Aloys that I would stay, as long as that remained the case. Some time later, President McCarthy approached my own professor, Charlie Dillon, in the hope of putting a stop to the affair. Charlie told him that he was very satisfied with every aspect of my teach-ing and research, besides being happy that I was able to oblige the Music Department by lecturing to their students. After every such Presidential outburst there would be a period of calm, in which I would quietly continue the lectures which took three hours a week of my time. Only Professor Fleischmann and myself were aware of the dramatic, almost farcical, background to the affair. We were careful to ensure that no hint of this would filter down to the students, who were, in general, enthusiastic about the Irish Music course and my participation in it.

I suppose I would have been in the Music Department for some two or three years when President McCarthy called Professor Fleischmann into his office, to tell him that he was withdrawing the small payment I was being made for giving the lectures. Aloys came to me in a distressed condition, wondering what he would do, since he had no funding to make up the shortfall in the Departmental cash. I told him that the money was not an important matter for me, as it had not been even mentioned in our original arrangement and was only granted after the lectures had been going for some time. He was very pleased to find that I was willing to continue without it, especially since, in his opinion, it was just another attempt by the President to have his way in the matter.

Normal life resumed and I continued with the lectures, until I was put into hospital for tests in January 1975. I had lost weight and it seemed my health was beginning to suffer from the strain of it all. I had earlier written to the President, seeking permission to go on an American lecture tour for the Irish-American Cultural Institute during the Easter vacation and had received his approval. Then a letter came to me from Dr McKiernan of the Institute, seeking to extend the tour slightly. It meant that I would be one day late in returning from America to UCC and would therefore miss the first day's lectures. I wrote to the President seeking his permission for this, expecting it to be a formality. I was amazed to get his curt reply, while I was in hospital, that he had given me permission to be away during the Easter vacation, nothing more. It seemed his original letter had been cut in stone.

For me, that was the last straw. I wrote to the President expressing my regret at his decision and letting him know that, in the circumstances, I had no option but to resign from the Special Lectureship in the Music Department. Unknown to me, my wife Helen went to see him in UCC and gave him a piece of her mind about his attitude and about the effect it was having. I understand there was quite a shouting match in his office. I wish I could have been a fly on the wall that day! President McCarthy was not used to people telling it like it really was, especially members of the opposite sex!

Professor Fleischmann rushed to the hospital next morning, in an attempt to get me to stay. I told him that I had had enough of the President's foolish games, but Aloys eventually persuaded me to return and complete the courses, so that the students would not be disadvantaged in their examinations. I agreed to remain until the summer. I enjoyed the reaction of the Governing Body when Aloys had the matter brought before them some time later: they decided that the President's earlier decision be rescinded and that I should be paid back the money due to me. I don't think Dr McCarthy liked that!

I must be destined to be continually at loggerheads with University Presidents. I spent a lot of time, while I was on the UCC Academic Council, being shouted at by Tadhg Ó Ciardha, a man with whom I normally enjoyed reasonably friendly relations outside the Council Room. My problem was that Tadhg treated the members of the Academic Council abominably: I always found it hard to come to terms with his bullying tactics in a forum that was supposed to include the top brains of the College. The problem was that many of them were in his debt, in University matters: an older University selection system had seen to it that jobs depended on much more than ability and the debt for past favours was a continuing one. I remember once trying to explain to a member of the Council that I felt it necessary to give expression to my belief that Tadhg's handling of the Council could not be allowed to continue without dissent. I was told that this only made him worse. My view, that it was necessary to let the council see this for itself, was not appreciated. I am obliged to record that Tadhg and I maintained cordial relations through it all, for, though he was a man of firm and sometimes fixed opinions, he didn't really hold grudges.

I had an on-going struggle with him in the early 1980s, when I tried to get a sabbatical to carry-out what I regarded as an interdisciplinary study on uilleann-piping, which involved travelling to do a survey of uilleann pipers in Ireland and America. He told me that the project wasn't interdisciplinary, which was a necessary point for him to make, since 'interdisciplinary' had become one of the 'in' University words at the time. However, it seemed that in the slightly 'Alice-in-Wonderland' world of UCC, the word 'interdisciplinary' meant only what Tadhg said it meant, so he stuck to his refusal. It took the Committee of Deans of the College to get him off the hook by suggesting the granting to me of a fellowship that was worth very much less than my salary. I think the hope was that I would refuse and the problem would thereby be solved in best Solomon style. For better or for worse, I took the money and ran all over Ireland and America for the next year.

While I was in America, I gave lectures and recitals to pay my way from piping centre to piping centre to complete the survey. It was ironic that North Eastern University in Boston, where I lectured, suggested the possibility of my going there for a year as lecturer in both engineering and music. My two-fisted approach to such academic disciplines was very attractive to them at the time, but I never took up their offer.

Part of my survey was an investigation of the traditional transmission of tunes and the effect of oral transmission on the actual tune-shapes. My method was to teach a tune to a player and ask them to transmit it to someone else, who would then pass it on in the same oral way, the tune being recorded at each transfer. I hoped, in this way, to establish some facts about oral transmission. The tune was a home-made reel – one of my own composition, in traditional style, called *The Reel Thing*. I think it was in Washington, after a lecture, that a lady asked me to teach her the tune and she would pass it on down the line. However, it seemed that she had missed the essential point of the experiment. She wrote to me a month later to tell me that she had taught it to everyone in her branch of the Comhaltas and they were playing it continually as a group ever since and liked it. What, she wanted to know, should they do next?

I had ambitious ideas about scientific tests of uilleann pipe chanters, with a view to establishing reed-making as a more exact science than it had been, but this never materialised, though I did assist students in the UCC Music Department on a similar project some years later. In all, I made contact, either face to face or by post, with some 200 pipers, who filled-up the questionnaire I had designed for the survey. One of the sections in that survey showed that Liam O'Flynn of *Planxty* was voted most popular piper, with Séamus Ennis, the famous Dublin piper, regarded as the most influential.

Quite a few years after the Irish Music affair with President McCarthy, and in the reign, as the *Bible* might say, of Tadhg Ó Ciardha, Mícheál Ó Súilleabháin, who was going on a sabbatical to Queen's University, Belfast, asked me if I would be willing to give the Irish Music lectures in his absence. Remembering my previous period in the Music Department, I told him that I would be pleased to oblige him, as long as it was cleared by the President's Office. He assured me that it was and I began the lectures. They were going well for some weeks, until a message from the President's Office said that they must cease forthwith, as they had not been authorised. I had to go into class and let the students know this. Their class representative decided to complain to both the Professor and the President. I sought an appointment with Tadhg, who told me it had not been sanctioned. As it happened, Mícheál rang him from Belfast while I was in the office. I could only hear one side of a two-sided conversation, which mostly consisted of Tadhg repeating: 'No you did not. I never sanctioned it.' I had to imagine the Belfast side of the exchanges. The upshot of the affair was that I was eventually allowed to continue the lectures, after the President and Mícheál had solved their differences. It was all a bit too much like UCC remembered, for my liking!

In more recent years, as well as being Dean of the Engineering Faculty, I have been in the Music Department, lecturing in Irish Music for the Folklore Department and in the Physics of Music, for the re-organised B. Mus. Giving the latter course, which was largely about acoustics, reminded me of my own B. Mus days, when Professor Fleischmann used to give a course on acoustics, based closely on Wood's book on the subject. The Professor warned me that he did not want to see me, *ever*, at his lectures on the topic, telling me that it was all from Wood's book, *The Physics of Music*, and that he, the professor, would be very uncomfortable with an electrical engineer, who would be expected to know all these things already, in his audience. I may point out that I was given no exam dispensation in the subject!

But life moves on: I took early retirement from UCC a few years ago, determined that I wouldn't join the serried ranks of University people there who just cannot break the link, even years after they are officially retired. I have stuck to my decision alright, but have weakened in another direction. The Cork School of Music started a BA degree in Music last year, in which I found myself teaching two courses, one an Introduction to Irish Traditional Music and the other on acoustics. I'll get sense yet!

SPAIN OF MY DREAMS

For longer than I can remember, Spain has been the country of my dreams. That started a long time ago and has been an ever-present in my life since then. Perhaps it was Franco, the man whom many Spaniards now confess to disliking, who was the indirect cause of it. When I was in Manchester, my companions in the house in which we stayed in Park Road were wont to put me in the position of defending the Catholic Church and everything attached to it whenever a discussion arose, no doubt because I was the sole Catholic in the half-dozen lodgers. Probably as a result of that I was trying to find a good argument to support the Franco/Catholic side in the Spanish Civil War. On a visit to Ireland, I got a few books on the subject from my former teacher, Br McFarland, who was a strong supporter of Franco. I don't remember if there was a winner in the debate in our house in Manchester on the subject, but I see it as the first step on my conversion to things Spanish.

At about the same time, there was an Advanced Maths teacher in Metrovick who gave it as his opinion that Spanish was the world language of the future and that young engineers like us might do well to take account of that fact. That this teacher turned out to be wrong in his assessment of the world language situation is not important: I had already made up my mind that I would study Spanish – somewhere, sometime. The somewhere turned out to be Liverpool, and the sometime was seven years later. I saw an advertisement for an extra-mural class in Spanish to be given by the Spanish Department of Liverpool University. I met a lady there who knew a Spanish fellow of my age, living in Liverpool, who was involved in the fruit import business. She wanted him to meet me, as she felt it would be good for his English and might help me in my Spanish studies.

She was right on both counts: Jaime Armero had recently completed his Spanish military service in Morocco and was now employed, or else about to be employed, by the Spanish Government in the fruit export business. Through Jaime, I got to know a network of people in Liverpool, all of whom were engaged in the fruit business. The advantage of this for me was that the group always spoke Spanish among themselves and encouraged me to do so too, even though my Spanish was, at first, pretty halting. It improved with time, especially after my first visit to Spain, when my brother and myself hitch-hiked across France and crossed the Spanish border in the back of a large fruit-lorry. My own memory of it is that we were almost suffocated on the journey, but my brother's chief recollection of it all is of my teaching him the verb 'to be' in Spanish, to prepare him for the year he was about to spend with the Marconi Española company there, doing graduate work in engineering. History shows that Aodh came back after his year in Spain a fluent Spanish speaker, with, as my mother observed, the Spanish habit of looking appreciatively after girls in town. I don't think my mother completely approved of that! I was impressed by the jump start the year in Spain had given his Spanish language ability and envied him that. I didn't actually decide then that I would spend a year in Spain sometime, but I was very aware that I would not get an easy fluency in the language without an extended period in the country. I had to wait some 30 years for that to materialise, but it did eventually – in 1989.

That was the year I got my second sabbatical leave from UCC, after having completed my first stint as Dean of Engineering. In those days there was no payment, either in kind or in cash, for the three quite busy years of a Deanship, with its commitment to meetings, conferences, student organisation, etc, but one had the option of applying for sabbatical leave and having a very good chance of getting it. I made previous arrangements with two Spanish institutions, the Universidad Politecnica in Valencia and the Universidad Politecnica in Madrid, to spend six months in each institution, during the calendar year of 1989. Thus it was that I set out with a car-load of goods and chattels in January, took the ferry from Rosslare to Fishguard, called

124

in to visit my friends, Bríd and Pat Crotty in Wales, took the car-ferry from Plymouth to Santander and drove down towards Valencia. The crossing from Plymouth had been calm – even after we rounded Brittany and that sharp top-left corner of France before entering the infamous Bay of Biscay, which has a name for rough seas. But not so that day. In fact, the complete 24 hour sea journey, which I had been dreading so much, was an absolute joy. That was partly due to some very pleasant company and stimulating conversation – 24 hours gives you plenty of time for that.

The exhiliaration of freedom that permeated me completely as soon as I got outside Santander was incredible and totally unexpected. I had surmounted the difficulties of negotiating city traffic on 'the wrong side of the road' and now the open highway stretched out in front of me. The day was bright and sunny and I wasn't due in Valencia until the following day, where I had a hotel booked for one night only. Every face I saw on my journey looked happy and so was I, for every choice was mine. I stopped at a wayside restaurant, making sure I parked the car where I could see it, since nearly everything I owned was in there, including my laptop computer and printer. As usual, it was a pleasant surprise to find again that my Spanish was able to cope with things, but then I had always kept it pretty well oiled, with live Spanish contacts on my amateur radio transmitter and frequent listenings to Spanish commercial radio stations. I ordered 'merluza' for lunch, because previous experience of Spanish fish-dishes told me that their hake was always tasty. Mind you, I was well aware that the harmless hake might have given up its life in Irish waters!

It was good to be under no real time pressure. I had already decided to look for accomodation for the night in Zaragoza, which was about halfway to Valencia. Spanish 'hostals' are not quite up to hotel standard, but are still government-controlled and they have a generally high standard of cleanliness and hygiene, with prices that are very reasonable. As some are better than others, there is an official grading system, but you can always be sure of a good minimum standard, even in the lowest grade. I booked into one in Zaragoza, complete with its own locked parking lot, so I didn't need to worry about my car-load of valuables. I breakfasted in a nearby restaurant because, like most hostals, this one did not have any eating facilities. Spanish toast – what they call 'tostado' – which is a half-fried, half-toasted slice of pre-buttered bread, is delicious. I got it that morning with Spanish coffee, which always seems to me much nicer than the French variety, and the inevitable peach jam. I knew I was finally back in Spain as I piled-on the jam and watched native Spaniards breakfasting. Even at that time of day some were contributing coins to gaming machines that answered them with musical jingles and a very occasional monetary jingle of winnings that drew the approval of the seated breakfasters.

The journey past Barcelona and down the East coast caused me no problems – that is, until I arrived on the outskirts of Valencia, only to discover that my hotel was on the other side of the city and I would have to make my way there in pretty horrendous evening traffic. I arrived eventually, checked into my room and phoned Kevin and Agnes Earley, an Irish couple whom Seán Teegan, a retired UCC colleague, had told me to contact. They were kind enough to offer me accomodation in their apartment until I could find a place for Helen and myself to live.

I went into the University next morning to meet my professor, Jose Luis Marin Galan, who gave me a warm welcome, to which I responded with a bottle of Irish whiskey, which pleased him a lot. We had a good chat about what was happening in the Department and what I could do there. We started and finished in Spanish, with the professor now and then dipping into English, when he would remind me that he would like to improve his English during my stay. He introduced me to the secretary of the Department, Roberta, whom we would get to know well during our period in Valencia, and to the members of the academic staff. I was to have my own desk in the same room as Dr Diez Caballeros, who was qualified in both medicine and engineering, which made him very useful in the Depart-

126

ment, where research was concerned with medical electronics. He was a big help to me when I started to translate my Control Engineering notes into Spanish.

I was then considered quite a fluent Spanish speaker, but I had never dealt with mathematical or technical aspects of the language. This meant that at first I couldn't express even the simplest basic control concepts in Spanish. My early days in Valencia were mostly concerned with this problem and I kept my laptop computer busy with a shiny new Spanish version of my Control Engineering notes, that just grew and grew! I even attended a series of research seminars in Artificial Intelligence, where I discovered something basic that anyone concerned with technical translation knows, ie, that technical language is in many ways only a collection of cliches that must be learned anew in each language. I was surprised at how well I could follow the Artificial Intelligence lectures after some preparation of basic vocabulary. It was, indirectly, a great help to me in preparing my own lectures.

All this time, I was paying 'through the nose' in a city-centre underground car-park for my Opel Ascona. I remained ten days to a fortnight with the Earleys before I secured accomodation. During that time I would go down to my car for a change of socks or shoes, underwear or a clean shirt, the back-seat being my changing-room. I had a small worry in the back of my head, all the time, that I would be robbed, but I am glad to say that it didn't happen. I began a systematic investigation of the summer apartments that were now empty, in the hope of getting something suitable. The more I saw of them, the more I realised that I didn't really want to stay in such places, which resembled deserted army barracks, far away from ordinary Spaniards.

On my way back from one of them, I followed a sign that indicated a small town called Sedavi, and when I reached it, I parked in the centre and asked two people emerging from a bank if they knew of anyone renting accomodation. They suggested that I try a man called Federico and gave me his address. He was not there, but his wife told me of a superior apartment that would be for rent soon. I made an arrangement to return and view the place next evening. Things were looking up at last. Federico's wife, Juanita, drove me to the village, Benetuser, to see the accomodation. It was on the first floor and proved to be a dream of an apartment, with most beautiful furniture and a large patio at the rear, with a magnificent flower-garden. I knew immediately that I had found the right place and I could imagine Helen's joy at being mistress of this wonderful abode for six months. There was only one snag, Juanita said, which was that the owner was not yet absolutely certain about letting it. We returned to her house in Sedavi, where she quizzed me about what I was doing in Valencia and enquired specifically what department of the *Universidad* I would be in. I told her, gave her my phone number and went away, hoping to hear from her very soon. I phoned again when I didn't get a call, but the story was still much the same. I had already agreed, of course, that I would be willing to pay the rent she was asking, which was high by their standards, but not by ours.

Next day in the university I was sauntering over to the restaurant for morning coffee when a couple greeted me. At first, I didn't recognise them, but then I realised that the lady was Juanita, accompanied by her husband Federico. They were a bit embarrassed, as their visit was for the purpose of checking that I really was a member of the university staff. They had intended, they told me, going to the professor to check my credentials, but were satisfied, now that they had met me, *in situ*, as it were! We agreed, there and then, that I could have the apartment, and we would arrange payment details when I moved in. Imagine my surprise to discover subsequently that the apartment actually belonged to Juanita's mother, who had, some time previously, moved with them to Sedavi, where they lived in a flat above that of Federico's aging parents. When I got to know Sedavi and Benetuser a bit better, I realised why their apartment had such wonderful furniture. Sedavi is known in Spain as *cuna del mueble*, the cradle of the Spanish furniture industry. Benetuser, too, has furniture-makers in every available small garage or room in the village.

128

One of the small factories near us in Benetuser manufactured hobby-horses and always displayed a selection of
them in their small shop-window, which was one of the
first stops for our Irish visitors, since it's not every day one
gets a chance to look at big hobby-horses, with beautifully
sculpted heads, alongside half-made hobby-horses, all
standing in a row – a most unusual sight.

Helen had come out from Ireland in time for the festival of Fallas and I was glad to be able to show her a buzzing
Valencia, preparing for its big occasion. She was, as I expected, thrilled with the apartment, but a little bit disappointed with Benetuser. She had expected something quite
different, more travel-guide type Spanish, with white
buildings overgrown with multi-coloured plants – the kind
of image that the very word *pueblo* conjures up. Benetuser,
while a genuine pueblo, as I had told her, with its own
mayor and council, seemed just a suburb of Valencia, with
few, if any, distinguished buildings. To add to the general
gloom, it was March and the people had not yet put on their
summer clothes, but we were soon to experience the warmth
and friendship of this close-knit community, when they got
to know the pair of Irish strangers who had landed among
them.

The big annual festival of 'Fallas' in Valencia, when
the town is ablaze with bonfires in every district, is really
due to the furniture industry. The original reason for the
bonfires was an attempt to get rid of all the surplus wood
that accumulated in the factories throughout the year. The
Valencians nowadays build huge effigies lampooning political figures, or topical events, with each district having
its own effigy and its fervent hope of winning the overall
prize. All of the huge figures, with one exception, are burned simultaneously on the Sunday evening nearest the feast
of St Joseph, patron saint of workers, while tumultuously
loud firecrackers rend the air and threaten the ear-drums.
On each of the days leading up to the festival, there is a
monster firework display at noon outside the City Hall, in
the centre of Valencia. I can't understand it myself, but
bangers and firecrackers seem to be of fundamental impor-

tance in Spanish life, especially around Valencia. You'll find them at churches too, for weddings, First Communions, feast-days and Confirmations. On the night of Fallas, all the city's firemen are on duty with engines running, ready to go to any situation of danger. There are certain places in the centre of the city where, because of the proximity of other buildings, it is necessary to keep hosing them all night. The only effigy which is not burned is the declared winner, which goes into the Fallas museum. A whole effigy-making industry has been built up over the years in association with the Fallas festival. One of the sad features of such events is that quite a few Spaniards have been killed by the fireworks. Even while we were there, a young fellow was carrying a big bundle of them, which exploded, killing him instantly and leaving a gaping hole in his side.

There is a tradition in the week of the Fallas that processions, with everyone carrying flowers, and accompanied by their own bands, make their way to the Plaza de la Virgen in the centre of Valencia and give up their flowers to men who, high up on a pyramid-shaped structure, topped by a head of the Virgin Mary which has real hair, begin to weave all the flowers into a glorious, multi-coloured cloak that eventually comes right down to the ground. The Plaza is bounded on one side by the Basilica of the Virgin and on another by the cathedral and is a favoured place, both for visitors who sip coffee in the surrounding cafés and for children feeding the many pigeons that find a home there. Helen discovered that when the Fallas finishes, on the Monday, anyone is welcome to take away as many of the beautiful flowers as they can carry – so she did! Attendance at the festival was a marvellous experience.

A large number of the residents of Benetuser and Sedavi were part-time farmers, with a few acres outside their village, where they would grow globe artichokes and other vegetables and fruit, including oranges. You would often see them in the morning, going by bicycle, with, perhaps, a dog in the basket behind them and a kind of basic spade tied to the bar of the bicycle. I remember one road leading out of

Benetuser on the way to the train-station, where the scent of orange blossom on an early Spring morning was a real joy.

There were acres of rice-fields just outside the village, which, in our earliest days, were bleak muddy moonscapes of no particular character. However, when the water was allowed to flow in through a complicated network of channels, the whole area took on a new beauty. Soon the rice would be pushing up through the water and the landscape would eventually become a vast sea of green. The management of its water resources was always important in the Valencian hinterland and there is a formal open-air meeting of the water tribunal every Thursday morning in the centre of the city. It is an ancient tradition with its own special ritual and we were privileged to have a special audience with the judge who presided over it – all arranged, of course by our friend and mentor, José Portales.

SPANISH CULTURE

Our apartment was at the very heart of Benetuser, with a school next door that had a chapel where we could attend morning mass, which we often did. The priest would ring the church bell about ten minutes before mass was due to begin and then once more, just before he'd start. The first bell was our signal to get up out of bed and the second bell told us that it was time to leave the house. Not a bad system, at all! Below us was a recreational centre for senior citizens whom you'd often hear playing cards and dominoes in the afternoon. They were not quiet placers of the cards: every one was laid down with a flourish and a shouted challenge to the opposition to do better. It was much the same with dominoes, which made a much bigger clack on the tables and seemed to cause even more excitement among the participants. Our back patio, with its flowers, was on the roof of the Centre, so we could monitor the downstairs activity while we watered the many exotic plants the owner had put there. Sitting under the warm evening sun could sometimes bring on a poem!

VALENCIA

Blundering in the sunset's afterglow above
My patio, radar guiding them to invisible flies,
The early bats swoop like apprentice swallows.

My neighbour's pigeon, craw swollen with grain,
Lands heavily on the balcony, waddles
Unashamedly to the pen, nosing the netting-wire
Door before her. From his ledge, the sleekid siamese
Watches both of us. The bird is too far
From his curved claws, so what does he want of me?

Cat, when I first heard your chilling
Cry in the warm night – that almost perfect
Musical third might have come from the mouth
Of a child who sang to show it wasn't frightened:
I hear it in nearly every dream and now
My wife has started yawning in your damned thirds!

132

Opposite us was the local Cultural Centre, where one could get a cup of coffee or a drink at any time of the day and meet the locals, who often played billiards – not really the same game as ours – and more cards. It was there we met the President of the Centre, José Portales, who invited us to attend the evening meetings, where someone would read a paper and discussion would follow. José lived just a few doors away from us. It was in the Centre that I first met a man who was to be an important part of our cultural introduction to the area – José Luis Vega and his girlfriend, Silvia. She was studying engineering and he was a newly-graduated teacher, full of enthusiasm for art, poetry and drama. When he discovered that I wrote poetry and played music, he asked if I could translate some of my poems and give a poetry reading/music recital in the Centre. He offered to give me any help that I needed with translation and so began a most productive collaboration that led to many visits to our apartment by both himself and Silvia. We learned a lot from each other, for he was very interested in things foreign and particularly in Ireland and its writers. He was soon helping me with the less technical parts of my Control Engineering lectures as well and I kept answering his queries about Ireland and its two languages. He even picked up some words of Irish, listening to Helen and myself conversing. Both José and Silvia were speakers of Valenciano, the Catalan dialect spoken normally by everyone in Benetuser. I picked up a little of it during our stay, but it was interesting to find that our speaking in Castillian Spanish, rather than Valenciano, marked us out as another type of stranger.

The series of lectures that José Luis organised in the Centre included the sort of Spanish topics one might expect, such as the writings of Blasco Ibañez, the prolific author of novels about the nearby lake, the Albufera, and its fishermen, but we also had talks on foreign writers, music, philosophy and nationalism. I gave my poetry reading and played Irish music on pipes before a big crowd, squeezed into the upper room of the Centre. When it was over, José Portales, on behalf of the Cultural Centre, presented me with a plaque, depicting three cultural Valencian figures, Blasco Ibañez, holding a book, composer Rodrigo behind a musical score and the painter Sorolla, with palette in hand and, below them, a sailing-boat on the Albufera. Portales gave a speech, welcoming us to Benetuser and saying how glad they all were that we had discovered their village. We had suddenly become a part of the *pueblo* and from then on, even the local chief of police went out of his way to tell me about impending traffic changes and to let me know which streets had even-date parking on which side. That was vital information in the narrow streets of Benetuser, where there was, as everywhere else in Spain, a tow-away scheme in operation against illegal car parking. We were also on first-name terms with the socialist mayor of the village.

It had been our intention to go to Seville for Holy Week, to see the famous ceremonies there, but our Benetuser friends didn't see why we needed to go to the south when they had their own Holy Week processions and ceremonies right there in the village, with a long tradition behind them as well – so we decided to stay. I remember, from my very first days there, a brother of Portales, himself a local Justice of the Peace and undertaker, showing me the exact spots on the road where Veronica would wipe Jesus' face with a towel and where He would fall the first and second time. We were given the special privilege of being taken up to a balcony above a furniture factory on Good Friday, where we had a grandstand view of the whole thing. Portales' brother had been right – every event of the carrying of the cross and the crucifixion took place exactly as he had predicted. The local band had an important part to play in the weekend ceremonies, with hymns, slow marches and the distinctive gliding walk that so matched the funeral music of Good Friday.

Even those implacably opposed to the Church came out for the Easter ceremonies, in the same way that they would come and stand outside the church while their children were receiving their First Communion inside. They always claimed that they and Spain were *muy Catolicos*, very

134

Catholic, but that did not mean that they felt any particular obligation to attend normal church services. Their obligation was to come and help the children to celebrate, with sweets, presents, a good meal and even a few firecrackers. Anyway, these were their friends, the actors who played the parts of Jesus, Mary, Veronica, Caiphas, Pilate and the soldiery – why shouldn't they come out and enjoy the spectacle?

Every facet of the Easter story was enacted on the streets of Benetuser: we had The Last Supper, The Agony in the Garden and the trial of Jesus by Pilate, which took place on a quickly-erected stage that we could see from our front room. The crucifixion happened outside the main church, which was about a quarter of a mile away from our house. The substitution of a statue for the real live Jesus who had just walked the streets of Benetuser, was cleverly done, just before the cross was raised into place, to be guarded by the soldiers. Equally clever was the taking down from the cross, later that day. It transpired that the figure of Jesus had hinged arms, so that as soon as the nails were removed, his arms could be put down by his side, thus allowing him to be carried quite naturally into the tomb for the interment.

On Easter Sunday morning we had the so-called 'meeting' of Jesus and Mary, with two separate processions, one with a statue of the risen Jesus and the other following a statue of Mary. They came together with much music, right outside our front door and the local pigeon club freed dozens of specially prepared birds to celebrate the event. They ascended in a blaze of colour, for the underside of each of their wings had been dyed by their owners – all in different colours. This impressive spectacle got sustained applause from an audience who knew exactly how it was going to happen, since they had seen it every other year. The various confraternities processed from different parts of the village, throwing sweets to all of us who were watching from the sidewalks, and mass was then celebrated on the platform, to finish Benetuser's Easter Week. For me, one important message coming out of the ceremonies was that here we had a closely-knit and interdependent community, which had a real pride in itself.

We set out for the south of Spain on Easter Monday, since the University was on holiday, and made our way down through the Sierra Nevada, which, true to its name, still had snow. We did a wonderful tour of Granada, Seville and Cordoba, stopping a night, or sometimes two in each place. We were in Seville on the Sunday after Easter and attended mass in the cathedral there. Afterwards we saw a procession forming and followed along. It was led by a priest carrying a monstrance containing the Blessed Sacrament, followed by altar-servers, a brass band and a crowd of 50 to 100 people. We stopped at various houses when there would be a musical salute from the band and the priest would carry the Blessed sacrament, on what we soon realised was a visitation to the sick of the parish. While he was inside, ministering to the sick, the marchers would open packets of cigars and cigarettes and the formal procession would be transformed into an informal chat and get-together of friends. As soon as the priest reappeared, smoking and chatting stopped and we were off again on our religious duties. It all finished with a short service at a small shrine in what looked, from the outside, like any ordinary garage, but was beautifully decorated inside.

We decided to set out for home straightaway and pointed the nose of the Ascona towards Valencia. It was a beautifully warm day, so I threw my leather jacket onto the back seat. The traffic leaving Seville was fairly heavy and we noticed one of those yellow motorbikes, so very common in modern Spain, weaving in and out around us, with two men on it. When we stopped at traffic lights, the pillion passenger got off and seemed to be looking for something at the roadside. We didn't pay too much attention to him, but drove on until we reached a petrol station and went in to fill-up, since such stations are not nearly so common in Spain as they are at home. We had to queue for petrol and noticed that the yellow motorbike had also come in and parked near us. Helen suddenly spotted the pillion passenger coming towards us and told me to close my window, which I did.

She told me later that she was afraid he was going to harm me. I looked at him approaching and made a sign to him not to come any nearer, to which he gave me a smile and an innocent shake of the head. Next moment he raised his arm and threw a stone which shattered our back window. Glass flew everywhere and, before we knew what was happening, he had reached in through the gaping hole, taken my leather jacket and was off at speed with his friend on the motorbike.

I was a bit shocked to discover that the staff of the garage and most of its customers seemed to be slightly amused at the incident, though I must say one woman, from behind us in the queue for petrol, came up to ask if we were short of money to pay for the petrol, as a result of what had happened. Fortunately, even though there had been money in the jacket, I kept most of our money in a belt, which was still intact. We rang the police, who came eventually and escorted us to a city-centre police station, where we were told to join about 20 others in a waiting-room. We could hear slow, laborious typing from the next room and every now and then a policeman would emerge and call someone in to the inner room. We had been there for more than two hours when he came out to tell us that they would see no one else that day, but would resume next morning. Everyone left quietly except myself and Helen. I knocked at the door to tell him that we had been brought there by the police and wanted an opportunity to report the incident. I must say that I expected to be told where to go, but he was actually very pleasant, if a little slow in his responses. He put new paper and about eleven separate carbons into his ancient typewriter and started to ask for details of our adventure in the filling station. I began to understand why each case had taken so long previously. When his investigation was complete, I tried to find out from him what I should do. The best he could manage was a rummage into the drawer of his desk, which resulted in the production of a business card belonging to a Seville firm which specialised in repairing smashed car windows. Obviously this was not a first!

I decided we had had enough of Seville for that day, so I covered the open window with cardboard and we set out for Cordoba, intending to stay the night there and seek an Opel garage next morning. We were lucky enough to find one that did the job satisfactorily before our drive back to Valencia. That city was looking much the same as when we had left it – as no doubt we were too, which shows that appearances can be very deceptive! Our Benetuser friends were sympathetic, but implied that if you were foolish enough to go down among those southerners, what could you expect? The local chief of police took more or less the same view, but seemed to increase the level of his benign protection of us strangers, from then on.

Our Seville adventure was not all a loss, however, as I gained a poem from it, which I called *Seville*:

An altar-boy with the sallow face of a Spanish
Saint swings a silver thurible, puffing
Incense along the street, into air already
Overburdened with the scent of orange blossom.

Holding his Saviour at arm's length, the priest
Nods for canopy-holders to protect his bald
Head from the sun and turns to bring the jagged
Monstrance into the final house of the sick.

One more time, the stopped band plays a quick
Salute to the Blessed Eucharist; then all light-up
Cigars: and altar-boys, in caps of ceremonial
Steel, are about to stop being saints.

Maria Ortega's sputtering candle smokes
In the shuttered bedroom, while she struggles to whisper:
   '*Señor*,
No soy digno ...': Lord, I am not worthy
That you should enter under my roof ...

Driving away from Seville, our car is buzzed
Again by the brazen Honda we can't
Shake off. At the petrol-station its pillion passenger
Jumps to slice the scented air with a stone

That makes a monstrance in jagged plastic
Of our car's back window. The pair of sudden saints
Accelerate away with my jacket, my money and are already
Half-way to Seville, still buzzing in the scented air.

The University changed its character a little, with the coming of the Summer term. The outdoor swimming pool opened and I often spent my lunchtime there, alternately swimming and drying myself under the bright sun, which was now shining every day. I began to feel that the *University Politecnica de Valencia* had something to offer that neither UCC nor any Irish institution could match. Speaking of Ireland, the Irish team had just beaten Spain at soccer – a most unusual event which I celebrated by pinning the result, without comment, on the door of my office. Some of my Spanish colleagues felt it was not in the best of taste!

I was to give a series of seminars on non-linear control in the Automatic Control Department beside us. I assumed the lectures were to be for final year students and had produced notes and overheads that would satisfy any student and, hopefully, leave him or her without the need to put too many technical questions in Spanish to me. The Head of Department said he would bring me in and introduce me to the class, which seemed to me an unusually formal approach to an undergraduate lecture. Imagine how surprised I was to find that my audience were staff members from the Department, with others from a sister-college. They were not shy about putting questions, of course, and I learned a lot of new technical Spanish trying to deal with them. In the process, we became good friends.

One of the unexpected aspects of the university was that each Department had its own patron saint and its own Feast day. All lectures and research were cancelled on that day and everyone was invited to partake of a paella, the most typical Valencian dish of all. Professor Marin Galan was at the head of the fun, stirring up the paella and reporting on its progress while others cut bread, prepared wine, or kept the fire going. This happened on the grassy lawn near the Department. It was an occasion for spouses too and Helen came along and met academic and technical staff and their partners. Spaniards are experts at enjoying themselves and the Valencians were no exception, letting their hair down and getting up to all sorts of capers. When their own Feast day was finished, Departmental staff cast eyes around for another Department's fun-day and tried to wangle an invitation there. In a place like the *Universidad Politecnica*, with a fair number of separate departments, one could look forward to such regular diversions in the summer term.

Encouraged by my friend José Luis, I began a frontal attack on the poetry of Antonio Machado and Miguel Hernandez. It was wonderful stuff and I was determined to use my time in Benetuser profitably, by learning some of it. José Luis introduced me to a couple of recordings by the Catalan singer Joan Manuel Serrat, who sang settings of the work of these poets. I was completely taken by Serrat's voice and his approach to the poetry. He also sang wonderful songs of his own about the poet Hernandez and his life. Miguel Hernandez had been imprisoned for many years in Franco's time and represented, for many Valencians and Catalans, their protest against the former leader. The singer, Joan Manuel Serrat, was interesting in his own right, for he had, some years before, been selected to represent Spain in the Eurovision Song Contest, but withdrew when the authorities would not allow him to sing in Catalan. The recordings of him that I admired were in Castilian Spanish, not Catalan, but while we were over there, he announced that all his future recordings would be in Catalan. I had hoped to hear him singing live, but he did not come to Valencia during our stay, though I was to attend a concert of his that autumn in Madrid.

With the approach of summer, the cultural evenings in the centre became outdoor events. About nine o'clock in the evening we would all be seated with our backs to the warm wall of the Recreational Centre next door to us, listening to the speaker, while the waiter from the Cultural centre moved among us, taking orders. There was no time-limit set on the proceedings, especially when one had topics that were close to the Valencian heart. I remember leaving one such evening about midnight and going up to bed. The debate still raged – and I do mean raged, for it concerned Lorca and the Civil War – for hours. I woke a few times to hear their impassioned arguments, wondering all the time that ordinary people could form themselves into serious discussion groups like this, in a small suburb of Valencia. I just couldn't imagine a suburb in Cork or Dublin taking matters of culture so seriously. There is something, not easily defined, in so many of the Spaniards that I have met, that inclines them towards cultural matters of both literature and art. It is one of the things that make me see them as a special race of people and one of the reasons that prompts me to say that Spain remains the country of my dreams.

That summer brought 100 visitors from Cork, for the orchestra of the Cork School of Music had an invitation to take part in a big celebration of Youth Orchestras, due to be held in the Palau de la Musica, the big concert-hall in the centre of Valencia. I was asked by Declan Townsend to play pipes in a composition of his for uilleann pipes and full orchestra. He sent me the music and I was ready for a practice-run on their arrival, but it didn't happen, as I shall shortly explain. Adrian Petcu rang me from Cork before they came, asking if it would be possible to arrange a public concert for the orchestra before the Palau appearance, to let his players get used to the new conditions. I mentioned the possibility to José Portales, who immediately suggested that the mayor, the Corporation and the Cultural Centre could combine to have an open-air concert in the square in front of the Town Hall. In no time at all José Portales had organised it all, including a big paella party for the orchestra beside the square. I arranged that they would all come up to our apartment afterwards for further refreshments. On the day of the first appearance of the orchestra, José bundled me into his car and we drove 30 miles to a Spanish school with Irish connections, so that he could bring back a huge tricolour to put on the stage. He felt it was only right that an Irish orchestra should show the Irish flag.

Suddenly it was nearing concert-time and the square was beginning to fill with people. The mayor was there and many important locals too. Violinist Séamus Conroy and trumpeter Mark O'Keefe had important solos with the orchestra and the crowd responded well. I went on stage a little nervously, but Adrian Petcu, who was conducting, gave me an encouraging smile and told me everything would be alright. My problem was that my solo entries were all clearly marked with A, B, C, etc, on my score, but I had no idea where those letters were in the main score. I sat so that I could see over the shoulders of the first violins and with a little help from them, came in at all the right moments. I enjoyed it much more than I expected and Adrian and Declan seemed delighted with the performance.

A big crowd assembled in our apartment afterwards and things were going well, until Portales suggested to me that the floors had not been designed to hold such a density of people. We quietly started moving our guests around, subtly I hope, so that, by spreading the load over the rooms and patio, the danger of us all disappearing into the Recreation Centre below was averted. The mayor and some of his friends started to dance and sing and we finished up with a great night. Cork seemed just a little nearer than it had been.

ADIOS VALENCIA! HOLA MADRID!

When our daughters Úna and Niamh arrived in Benetuser on holidays, they caused quite a romantic flutter among the local young fellows, who used to assemble at our door and wait for them to come out. One of them fancied himself as a good English speaker and a shade superior to the rest of his friends. In response to their knock, Helen opened the window and looked down to see who was there. The lad I have mentioned stepped forward and said something which Helen did not understand. She summoned up her best Spanish and said to him: *lo siento, no te entiendo*, at which the other lads burst out laughing, for she had just told him in Spanish that she didn't understand him – and his fame as an English speaker was at an end!

My cousin Harry Coyle and his wife Winnie came out for the last week of our stay and we had a great time. Helen persuaded Winnie, who had an inordinate fear of water, to come into the sea with her at Cullera and, much to Harry's surprise, she did. There was no stopping her after that and we used to go every day to the local pool, where Winnie learned to swim – and gave me the credit for teaching her. On my last night in Benetuser, the locals had organised a big open-air paella supper, to which they invited Harry and Winnie. They were disappointed that Helen was already booked to return to Cork the previous day. After supper, there was a sing-song, to which Harry, Winnie and I contributed. Since there were just the three of us and we had all sung, our Benetuser friends wanted to know if every single person in Ireland could sing like us!

Then they surprised me with a big sketch of myself, magnificently mounted and framed. It was a surprise because, even though I had done a sitting for the artist in his home, some miles away, a month previously, they had got me there under false pretences. The story was that this artist, originally from Benetuser, wanted to draw an Irish musician, holding his musical instrument and could I possibly oblige him. I did, of course, and this presentation picture was the result. I was very moved by the gesture and said so in my acceptance speech, thanking them for their friendship, which meant so much to Helen and myself. Just to show that I had learned something from them during my stay, I concluded with a few words in Valenciano!

Next day, after seeing Harry and Winnie off at the airport, I turned the snout of my Ascona west and aimed for what was to be our new home – Madrid. Harry had kindly volunteered to take the very large picture to Derry with him and I was to pick it up there later. I felt a bit guilty about the inconvenience it might cause him on the journey, but he made light of it and I took him at his word. All my worldly goods had been re-packed into the car, which encouraged me to start worrying again about car thieves and such-like, as I drove into the sun over the high central plain that had Madrid as its centre-point. Just as I had done on my first days in Valencia, I left my overloaded car in an underground car-park and walked up the Gran Via, looking for a reasonable hostal, which I soon found.

That hostal, in a side-street off the Gran Via, was to be my base until I could sort out an apartment for Helen and myself. For the first few days, I wasn't having much success, even though a Spanish resident, Javier Escribano and his wife Carmen, good friends of my brother, were helping me. One day I mentioned my problem to the landlord, Urbano, with whom I had become quite friendly. He told me that they had a few apartments for rent and one of them had that day become available. We made our bargain and I became the tenant of a third-floor apartment on Calle Montera, right beside the red-light district of Madrid and only a few yards from the Puerta del Sol, which is considered, from a geographical point of view, the very centre of Spain. Set into the pavement there, just outside a barracks, is the marker from which all Spanish road distances are measured.

A big difference between Benetuser and Madrid was concerned with car parking. There was no local police-chief

144

here to keep me right about it and parking, even for a few minutes outside our new apartment, was out of the question. The hungry *grua*, the lorry that shifted illegal parkers, continually roamed the streets.

Madrid was clearly going to be a quite different experience from the semi-rural life we had lived in Benetuser. The new apartment was not a patch on our Valencian accomodation and cost much more, with just one main bedroom, containing a double bed, until Carmen loaned us a fold-away model, which would be useful for visitors. While attending a show at a nearby theatre on my first night in residence, I was obliged to come home at the interval to put on a jumper, since the building was air-conditioned and consequently much colder than on the streets. I strolled slowly back to the theatre then and was in plenty of time for the second act of the play, which made me realise that Calle Montera had some advantages.

Helen came out from Cork again and we started another home in the new flat, with a balcony overlooking Montera and its pick-pockets and touts of every variety. We'd often sit there in the evening, watching the action below, regretting that we were too far away to shout a warning to unsuspecting tourists who were about to be robbed by a pair of locals, whose intentions were so obvious from our lofty position. At other times you would see police chase drug suspects, who might throw away something as they ran. After they had captured him or her, the law would return and look for missing evidence under every car and in every doorway on the street.

Montera must have been one of the noisiest streets in Madrid, with a continual stream of taxis making their way back empty, after depositing passengers in the heart of the Gran Via. This meant that we had a magnificent personal taxi-service at our front door, day and night. Talking about night, it was not always easy to get to sleep in our new apartment. At first, you would hear the crowds coming out of late-night shows, happy and chattering beneath our window. There would be a lull then, before the dustbin-men came clattering bins and boxes, shouting to each other. A little sleeping time then before a special group of refuse-collectors picking up discarded cardboard from the various shops on the street, wakened us up again and we were hardly settled before the street-cleaners came with their power hoses and shouted conversation. Notwithstanding all the noise, we soon acclimatised and hardly noticed it.

At the University I met my new boss, Professor Puente, in the Control Department. He was busily preparing for an international engineering conference that the University was to host the following month and asked if I would be willing to help them with it, particularly since the language of the conference was English. I readily agreed and one of my first jobs was to write the opening speech of the conference, to be delivered by the President of the University. I never actually met the man face to face, so it was quite eerie to listen to him, a month later, saying my words and using my turns of phrase in welcoming the international delegates. He took their applause without any shame whatsoever and I knew then how government ghost-writers must feel!

I soon discovered that I could get a bus from Puerta del Sol to the door of the University on a regular service that was not expensive, so my car had become redundant. When I got a permit and permission to park at the University, that institution became my academic home, as well as my parking lot. From then on, I would shift the Ascona only for special excursions to such well-known places as Escorial or Aranjuez. The latter was an extremely beautiful place, with gorgeous gardens and a palace that was once the summer residence of the kings of Spain. Royalty seems to be good at picking the best spots for itself – it was ever so. The famous *Concierto de Aranjuez*, by Joaquín Rodrigo, while a marvellous piece of music, is not more beautiful than the enchanting place that inspired it.

Madrid is a most attractive city, with more green spaces than any European capital, and we enjoyed exploring it. We lived only a short walk away from the Retiro Park, where, on a Sunday, you could find buskers, tarot-card readers and dancers of every nationality, or go for a trip in a boat on the lake. Near the Retiro is the Picasso museum, where that famous artist's large and much-talked-about Guernica picture is the sole exhibit and, of course, only a few hundred yards away is the world-famous Prado Art Gallery, which we visited on a few occasions.

We saw many plays and shows during our time in the Spanish capital. As well as professional productions, there were often shows held in banks and main post-offices, where there was no admission charge. We would often walk along Recolletos Avenue to get to the underground complex in Colon that contained a number of theatres, to which you gained entry by going under a tremendously high and powerful waterfall. We saw some marvellous shows of Flamenco there and heard fine poetry readings. We would sometimes call in to the Café Gijon, which José Luis had told us about – the one that used to be frequented by all the top Spanish writers in pre- and post-civil war days. It was still very much aware of its own importance and the waiters would size you up, before condescending to serve you. Most definitely *the* place to be seen in! The Lope de Vega Theatre was quite near and we saw some fine medieval plays there. I remember one in particular that was presented in a surrealist way, with human trees that raised umbrellas from which tinsel hung in streamers, to indicate rain. Near the same district was the big Bellas Artes building, where for a small extra fee you could drink coffee in glorious comfort and stay as long as you liked. In a nearby theatre we saw the show which had recently been such a box-office success in Barcelona, *Cielo y Mar*, a kind of musical, with outstanding stage effects, and, in the same theatre, sometime later, I listened to my favourite Spanish singer, Joan Manuel Serrat.

It was easy to saunter from our flat down to the Plaza Mayor, where there were cafés and shops galore, surrounding the central open space. You could find just about everything in the shops: some of them were specialists in stamps, while others dealt exclusively in cloth of every colour, to cater for the different confraternities. Below the Plaza Mayor itself there were more cafés, set into caves. One of them had a big notice in the front window, saying: 'Hemingway *did not* eat here'! On the way back from the Plaza one evening, our curiosity took us into an art gallery, where we followed a crowd we should not have followed and finished up enjoying a quite sumptuous spread of food and wine, to which we had no entitlement. These things require 'neck'.

I had a sad phone-call one day in Madrid, telling me that my friend Crookie, drummer in the Liverpool Ceilí Band, had died.

DRUMMER OF THE FIVE LAMPS

A voice from Cork to Madrid tells me, Crookie,
What cannot be – that no drumhead will again
Respond to your pulsing sticks; no drumhead delight
In the singing shiver of its quivering skin. I thought
A drummer could not die, that all the years
Of rolling into marches and tip-tapping a wayward
Liverpool Band towards jigs and reels would keep you
Vibrating, long after our miserable oscillations
Had dampened, like ourselves, into earth. I should have
Put the damned phone down earlier and just listened,
To hear again out of the hollow of years, music
From the Five Lamps of Waterloo, with Peggy's
Taut piano-chords in my left ear
And in my right, Crookie, the heartbeat
Of your side-drum, regulating my errant fingers.

One of Madrid's best-known landmarks is the Rastro open-air flea-market, which opens on a Sunday, and whose stalls in the main street and side-streets stock just about everything you could possibly want. We went there to see what was to be seen and discovered that our Calle Montera experience stood us in good stead. Helen, walking behind me in the crush, noticed a man with a jacket over his arm, making his way towards me. The jacket over the arm is the Spanish pick-pocket's chief weapon, allowing him to use his other hand, covered by the jacket, to unobtrusively continue his vocation. Helen's alarm systems were working well and she pulled his hand away from my hip-pocket. He just looked at her and walked away: being caught in the act is not something that disturbs them unduly. Calle Montera had prepared us for that fact, too.

Shopping was one of Madrid's pleasures, whether it was for fruit and vegetables in the basement of the Corte Inglés or for fashion in one of the many big stores, within a few hundred yards of our apartment. We began to feel proud of the facilities of our adopted city, as we escorted our visitors around it. Frank Deeney, a school friend of mine, and now a priest in England stayed with us for a week and changed our routine by offering daily mass with us in the apartment and bringing us to a number of beautiful churches we had never seen before. My cousin and godmother, Kathleen Coyle, helped us to discover places that made good hot chocolate, which is a fine drink for making you feel warm and putting you in a reminiscent mood. I am told alcoholic liquor has similar powers! A Cork friend of ours, Mary Murphy, came out to visit us and insisted that we find the local swimming pool, so that she could tell her friends that she had been swimming in Spain on her holidays. It was all good fun and a period of our lives that we won't forget, but our Spanish sojourn was coming inexorably to its end.

Looking back on the sabbatical, our decision to settle in the village of Benetuser was probably the very best thing we had done all year. Madrid is a fine city, of course, with all the amenities one could desire, but there was no way we were going to get to know Spanish people there, in the way that we had in Benetuser. In our six months in that village we had experienced the very heart and pulse of the area and its people, in a rewarding and enriching contact that was unique – there is no other word for it.

Christmas was on its way and the Corte Inglés had its annual Don Quixote and Sancho Panza representation high up on the walls of the store, with a steed that moved its head and made animal noises in response to its master's voice. Above him were the giants and below them a huge crib, surrounded by shepherds and goatherds. When the clock struck the hour, everything would begin to move to the music and hymns, coming out over the loudspeakers.

Of course, Christmas made us think of home and we started to prepare for another shift – this time to Ireland. Helen had left Valencia before me and we had planned the same move for Madrid, but a late change in the ferry schedule from Santander to Plymouth meant that I set out in the Ascona a day before Helen, leaving her to spend the last night in Madrid, alone in Calle Montera – something that she was a little worried about at first, but all worked out satisfactorily in the end. I called to see our good friend Inés Praga in the University of Burgos, which was on the road to Santander, where I would catch the ferry for Plymouth. Helen, meanwhile, got a plane home next day, and I made a slow return via England and Annamakerrig to Cork and the old realities!

THE MIDDLE EAST

My first contact with the Middle East was when I went there on an international control engineering conference in 1967, just after the completion of the six days war between Israel and Egypt. It had looked for a while before this as if the war would interfere with our get-together of engineers, but it didn't. My job in Haifa was to present a paper on research that we were doing in UCC and I welcomed the opportunity of seeing modern Israel. My interest in the language had been nurtured in Liverpool, with Hebrew lessons from two Israeli research students there. When I stepped off the plane, I was given a fulsome greeting by one of the conference organisers, who wondered if I was a long-lost Jew! My name, Ó Canainn, was so very like the Israeli name Canaan that he was sure I was his brother in religion. To make up for any disappointment that he might have felt on that score, I let him know that I was an admirer of their language revival policy. I even remembered the *mazal tov* greeting from the days of my Liverpool lessons.

After introductory speeches by various dignitaries, the conference proper began and various technical papers were presented by the international body of participants, myself included. One aspect of the affair was quite disturbing for some of us – the obvious intention of the Israeli organisers to exert a certain political influence on everyone. We were shown newsreels from the media with Nasser, the Egyptian leader, frequently included, to the accompaniment of much booing from the locals. This was bad enough, but when they brought in an army colonel to give us a talk on how they had won the war, I couldn't take any more. I stood up and said that I objected to such a presentation, which had no place at a scientific conference. The President of IFAC (International Federation of Automatic Control), Englishman Professor Coales, was on his feet immediately, to tell his Israeli hosts how much the Federation appreciated their co-operation in organising the conference in such diffi-cult circumstances. The same professor was noticeably less friendly to me subsequently!

I had always wanted to visit an Israeli kibbutz, so as soon as the conference finished I travelled to Telaviv, where there was a hostel, which acted as a kind of clear-ing-house for kibbutzim volunteers. I was to spend a night there and go next day to the particular kibbutz to which I had been assigned. It was called Alumot and was situated high on a hill on the shores of Lake Genasereth. I went to bed early in a small four-bedded dormitory and was just dropping-off to sleep when a couple of very talkative Eng-lish lads came in. After they got into bed, they started a conversation about some 'lovely birds' they had seen that day and it was pretty clear that they felt a pressing need for female company. At long last they quietened and went to sleep. Much later, I was awakened by the sound of the door opening and someone entering. Even in the half-light, it was obvious that the newcomer was a girl, who quickly slipped off her clothes and got into the empty bed on the other side of the room. The two English lads just kept on snoring!

When I awoke next morning, the lady had gone. The landlord told me at breakfast that she had used the hostel some weeks before and on that occasion the small dormitory had been assigned to girls, which explained our intruder's presence. My English friends were not inclined at first to believe my story of our night-visitor and when I eventually convinced them, they wanted to know why I had not wakened them!

The couple I stayed with in Alumot were long-time resi-dents of that kibbutz. In fact, the lady's father was one of the original founders and still lived there. The couple would go out working every day, she with cattle, while he toiled in the fields. We all dined communally in the even-ing, though all the children of the kibbutz were kept to-gether, even at meals, away from their parents. It was only at the weekend that they were reunited as a family. All the business of the kibbutz was run by a committee, on which my hosts served. As well as organising work-schedules, they dealt with security – a very sensitive area in every kibbutz – and with deciding who should be allowed into permanent membership. There was one visitor who had been there for a considerable time and was very keen to join, but they constantly refused her, as she had a health problem, which they reckoned could be a burden on the kibbutz. Apart from the undesirable expense involved if the girl's health deteriorated, all members of the kibbutz were, in reality, a part of the kibbutz security army and they couldn't afford passengers in that department.

I had promised to go to Jerusalem to visit an Arab engineer who had been at the conference. When I arrived, he took me on a tour of 'The Holy City', showing me the wailing wall, which is all that is left of the Jewish temple, and the big Arabic mosque with its golden dome. We both took off our shoes before entering the mosque. My friend was very angry that triumphalist Jews were crowding in, without removing footwear, thus failing to show respect for this most holy shrine of Islam. The fall of Jerusalem in the recent war had been, for him and his people, as big a defeat as it had been a victory for the Israelis.

I had gone to Israel a convinced supporter of its people and all that they stood for, but I left it an equally convinced supporter of their sworn enemies, the Arabs, who seemed to me a quieter, friendlier race, having more in common with the Irish than the stiffer, strident Israelis. I had an opportunity, some ten years later, to find out more about other Arabs in a different country, when I was asked by the Cultural Relations Committee of the Irish Department of Foreign Affairs to give a lecture at the Babylon International Festival in Baghdad, on possible relationships between Arabian and Irish music. With impeccable timing, the Festival opened just a few weeks after the end of the Iraq-Iran war. I couldn't help wondering if I was doing the right thing, but I went anyway.

All the foreign lecturers travelled from London on a specially chartered plane that arrived in Baghdad in late afternoon. I was surprised to be met at the baggage collection area by the first secretary of the Irish embassy, John

Rowan, who escorted me past a long queue, waiting for a security and customs check. We were nodded through, to the surprise of my fellow-lecturers from Britain and America and then whisked away to the top hotel in which we were to stay. Some of the other delegates were a bit miffed that their own embassy staff had not come to assist them, particularly when a small country like Ireland could show-up for their single representative! Later that evening, the Irish ambassador, Pat McCabe, brought me to the Minister of Culture, who was directing affairs at the Festival, for a discussion on my lecture. It soon transpired that the organisers intended that no paper should exceed fifteen minutes reading time. The Irish ambassador pointed out firmly that I had prepared a paper which would last 45 minutes and there was no way it could be shortened. I was asked to confirm this, which I did. There was then a long session of what I can only call political and cultural circling which I thought had reached no result, with both sides sticking by their original positions. The whole thing was conducted in a most civilised fashion, with no raised voice or anger, but we said goodnight and left with, as I thought, nothing accomplished. I could not understand why the ambassador seemed satisfied that he had made his point. He asked me to meet him in the morning before the conference opened and told me not to worry about it.

We sat side by side at the main conference table next day, with a microphone and intercom at each position and a bevy of television cameras in the background. There was simultaneous translation of the proceedings – you just put on the headset and turned a knob to give your required language. After the conference was opened by another minister, the Festival Director stood up to explain the order of business. Each speaker, he said, would be allowed fifteen minutes to deliver his or her paper and this would be followed by questions. He emphasised how important it was that each contribution be limited to the stated time. I was trying to decide what parts of my lecture I would jettison and what I should keep, when I heard him say: 'Keeping to this time limit is vital, except, of course, in the case of the Conference

Opening Address by Dr Ó Canainn, from Ireland.' Pat McCabe looked at me and said nothing. I stood up and launched into the lecture. After about ten minutes Pat slipped me a note which read: 'Keep going – you're winning!' End of first lesson on international diplomacy! I got good attention, especially when I played pipes or sang, to illustrate a point. At the end, the Director put his arms around me and everyone was happy. Honour had been satisfied on all sides and there was no loser in the small political confrontation. That was important in the situation.

Next evening I switched on the TV in my bedroom to find myself in picture, playing pipes. I was tickled to see that they had kept a clip of that. When I reached the end of the tune, I expected the news announcer, or whoever was presenting the clip, to change to another topic, but they did nothing of the kind. Instead, the piper stood up and continued his lecture, overdubbed in Arabic by the instant translation system. Luckily, I had given them a full copy of the lecture. I was amazed that a complete lecture on a cultural topic would be carried on the normal TV channel! My big regret, since I started to study Arabic myself, is that I didn't get a copy of the video then. I'd be next best thing to a native speaker of Arabic by this time, if I had!

John Rowan took me down to the *suk*, or market, in Baghdad next day. It was a most intriguing place, full of artisans in copper and wood. We watched an old man making intricate designs on copper and John said something complimentary about his work. He looked up, spotted me and began to talk excitedly, pointing me out to other stall-holders. John explained that he was telling them I was Irish and that he had seen me playing a wonderful Irish musical instrument. What friendly people these Arabs were. I was famous!

There were fine evening shows at the Babylon Festival outdoor platform, especially those that involved music from Iraq itself, for they had outstandingly good performers, particularly on lute and a kind of native violin. On our way into the concerts, we could see a holographic display in the sky above our heads depicting Sadam Hussein, accompanied by a major figure from their history – Nebucchad-nezzar. The message of Sadam's quasi-immortality was quite clear from this 'heavenly' electronic show. As far as one could judge, he was a popular leader of his people, for every shop in Baghdad, big or small, had its colour-picture of Sadam on the wall.

On another visit to the Middle East some years ago, I saw a different side of the Arab personality when I stop-ped-over in Cairo, on my way to Jordan for an engineering conference in Amman. From my hotel window I could see an officer putting a company of soldiers through their paces. If any soldier failed to complete the requisite number of press-ups, he would get a series of lashes from the whip that the officer carried. One of the offenders couldn't stand the whipping any longer and ran off, followed by the officer, still lashing out at him.

I had a further contact with the Egyptian army when I was trying to find the Cairo Museum. I asked a soldier on guard-duty outside a big public building if he could tell me where it was. His reaction surprised me. I have always had a bad habit of keeping money in the top pocket of my jacket and, a short time before, had pushed a few Egyptian notes in there. The soldier didn't answer my query about the museum, but reached out the hand that wasn't holding the rifle and started to take my money. Rifle or no rifle, I was determined he was not going to get it, so I gripped his wrist and he released his grasp on the notes. I have to say that I was shocked that a soldier on official guard-duty would do such a thing. For me, it was just one more indication of the low standard of living suffered by so many arabs. Going around the streets of Cairo, I was besieged by beggars, every one of them communicating their request for money with the single word – *baksheesh*. It was a word I came to hate, for it seemed almost the badge of these people's bondage. Unfor-tunately, requests for *baksheesh* were not confined to what one might regard as professional beggars. The boatman who took me sailing on the Nile felt obliged to slip the offend-ing word between us, even after he had been well paid for the trip. In the end, I began to wonder if there was some element of a 'them' and 'us' ethos in all of this – an inverted pride in their low station and a determination to keep the stranger at arm's length, to establish boundaries.

MY LOVE-AFFAIR WITH RADIO

I have always had a love-affair with radio, one way or another. I suppose it started when I began to make crystal sets in cocoa boxes at about twelve years of age. The thrill of moving the cat's whisker on the crystal until music or voices came crackling in on the earphones was unforgettable. But I still can't explain why the sounds seemed to occur in my throat, rather than in my ears: it was all part of the mystery that was radio. Winding the tuning coil was an inexact science, when you hadn't any idea of how many turns might be needed on a big box, if 50 had been right for a small one previously. It was a splendid training in experimental science! We would often find usable radio parts on the big heaps of discarded equipment that lay on the quayside in Derry, in the days when British and Canadian naval destroyers lined the docks. They were the fleet that guarded the so-called north-west passage and kept it clear of submarines for the convoys.

I was aware, even in those days, that there were amateur radio operators in Derry who were in contact with the world, from transmitters in their own houses – something that seemed to me quite magical. I was not conscious of it at the time, but I am sure another small radio seed was thus sown in my brain. It took some ten years to germinate but bore fruit eventually when I took out my own radio licence and made my first contacts. In the beginning it was with morse code and later with speech. Morse is something I don't often use nowadays, but it always stays in my mind and I often find myself translating notices and signs into morse code. I have even been known to interpret pigeon-cooing in the early morning as if it were a morse signal to us! On a recent holiday, I established that pigeons in Athens were sending non-stop messages of the letters AR, AR, AR. I am sure such heartfelt utterings have deep significance for Greek pigeons at six o'clock of a winter's morning!

Our daughters still talk of the time my amateur-radio interest was concentrated on RTTY – a kind of teleprinting, with the signal coming into my receiver in a series that was, for the unitiated, not unlike morse. My equipment would convert these signals to work an ancient teleprinter, known in the business as a Creed 7B. What a noise it made in our small house at that time! We lived on the Douglas Road in a bungalow that had what I might call a half-storey upstairs. My clonker of a teleprinter was in the roof-space beside the girls' bedroom, spewing long-winded messages on rolls of paper. It was exciting to receive commercial RTTY from Russia, complaining about the decadent American Peace Corps of that time, and equally virulent anti-Russian propaganda from the news agency, Reuter, in the next transmission. But individual personal communication with other amateurs like myself, across the world, struggling to keep their equipment working, was most satisfying of all. The Cork Radio Club had a meeting in Collins Army Barracks once, at which I was to give a talk on RTTY. Getting my Creed 7B up there in one piece and making it work was no small victory.

When I was receiving a message at home in the early days, the house would shake and no one could sleep – I was not popular, that is until I discovered the magic of three inch deep foam! Put under the teleprinter, it completely damped the vibrations, thereby saving my bacon and going some way to restoring family unity!

I was pleased to make my amateur radio hobby work for my friends, maintaining contacts with people abroad. Such a case occurred when Fr Michael Ryan was transferred to the Cork mission in Peru. I had known Michael when he was a curate in the parish of our Lady Crowned in Mayfield, during the period I was in charge of the choir there, so I was determined to establish the link again. I contacted a radio amateur in Lima one Sunday and they promised to have another operator from Trujillo, where the mission was based, on frequency the following Sunday at the same time. I made the contact alright and the man from Trujillo said he would try and get Fr Michael up to his place next day, which he did. Apart from the excitement of making the contact with a surprised Michael, the project was good practice for my South-American Spanish. We had a regular schedule after that, passing news from Cork and getting the latest from Trujillo. We once had some urgent messages, to-and-fro, about a priest out there who was ill and was being transferred back to Cork.

I decided to bring Michael's parents, whom I knew well, from their home in Watergrasshill to our house on an evening that I was to contact Michael. They sat in the small room where I had the transmitter and were transported into seventh heaven when they heard the voice of their favourite son, after such a long absence. Michael and I usually spoke Irish on these occasions, as he did not wish the locals in Peru to know every detail of the business of the mission. On this occasion, however, we changed into English. I am reminded of another occasion when Michael's parents brought with them a friend, Jim Sarsfield, who had recently been elected to the Cork County Council and knew Michael very well. He was quite a comedian, in his own right. As soon as he heard Michael's voice from Peru, he took the microphone from me and shouted into it: 'Hello der, Michael boy, I've just been elected to the Council, so if any of your Peruvian friends want a road tarred by the Council or a hen-house built, just tell them to get in touch with me, Jim Sarsfield: I won't see them stuck!' I didn't know what to do, for this was all highly illegal and could cause the loss of my licence if any of the authorities were listening, but it was worth it for sheer enjoyment.

One other time, just after we had completed our contact, I got a call from a radio amateur in New York. He told me that he was of Irish descent and had been listening to our conversation. Even though he couldn't understand, he knew that it was Irish, so we finished up chatting about Ireland, the language, uilleann pipes and traditional music, in which he had a great interest. He asked me to translate some words of a song that he had on an Irish tape, which I did without much trouble, as it was one I often sang. He read me out details of the tape then and was surprised to hear that the group on the record, *Na Filí*, were from Cork and I was the singer and piper. We kept in touch after that and I met him on a subsequent visit to New York. I was not a little surprised to hear that he had, subsequent to our radio contact, joined an Irish class in New York and his son was learning pipes from a good friend of mine over there, piper Bill Ochs. It is very, very definitely a tiny, tiny, world. As the Spaniards say – *el mundo es un pañuelo* – the world is a handkerchief!

I was in contact with the Vatican on amateur radio once. The amateur station there was run by the Jesuits and this was reflected in their call-sign. Every station has its own call-sign: mine is EI7AV, where the EI lets other amateurs know that they are talking to an Irish person and the 7AV is the identification issued to me by the Post Office. One normally gives one's call-sign at the beginning and end of each contact. I usually say something like 'Echo India Seven Alpha Victor', so the first letter of each word identifies my station. The Vatican station I spoke to was, I think, HV3SJ, where SJ stood for Society of Jesus, the official title of the Jesuits and HV were the identifying letters for the Vatican. The particular Jesuit on the microphone that day must have had a wry sense of humour, for he was calling out, somewhat irreverently, 'HV3, Strawberry Jam'. I contacted him and we had a nice long chat.

I narrowly missed a contact on another occasion with the King of Jordan, who is a keen radio-amateur, but I consoled myself with a refreshing chat with Bernie O'Sullivan, who came on frequency. Bernie lives on the Beara peninsula and knows more about the area than any king knows about his kingdom! It was Bernie who took me around that area once, when I was collecting songs for a book of mine, *Songs of Cork*. One of the singers he introduced me to was Joe Murphy, who had written one of the songs himself. I think it was about the local, Urhan football team, for whom Joe had once played. After he had sung it, I asked him was it a local song. 'Yes', was the answer. When I asked ed him if it was very local, he laughed and agreed, shyly, that it was very local indeed!

I have been involved with many commercial radio programmes over the years, giving talks on RTE's *Sunday Miscellany*, *Living Word* and guesting on other ones, like Ciarán MacMathúna's *Mo Cheol Thú*. I enjoyed them all and each one was a different challenge. I always found the BBC refreshing, whether in London, Belfast or Derry, where they even have programmes in Irish that I have spoken on. Equally refreshing were chats on 96FM or RTE with Eilís Geary, or with Dan Collins on Radio Kerry. Particularly enjoyable were various programmes on Radio na Gaeltachta, which always seems to me to be closer to its audience than any station I know.

My longest radio involvement was with a programme from Cork every Saturday morning for a few years. It was mostly known as *Móra Dhíbh*, though it had other names during the time I presented it. I had been asked to do it by the Head of the local station, Uinsinn MacGruairc, for whom I had recorded a number of interviews previously. It was part of my job to provide a list of records, with timings, for the sound-desk operator, but apart from that, the whole affair was free and easy, which pleased me a lot, as I like live radio without a script. The programme, mostly but not exclusively devoted to Irish traditional music, began at half-past seven on a Saturday morning and finished at nine o'clock, with a break for the eight o'clock news. That was the time we would partake of breakfast, with half an ear cocked for the progress of the news, just in case we were required in an emergency. The programme always got a good reaction, particularly when I started a series of mostly pre-recorded interviews, using my own Grundig recorder. Deirdre Davitt came on the programme for a while, to do alternate months with me, as we were on a month's contract in those days.

Uinsinn left his job as Head of the station and went for a while to be *Ceannaire* of Radio na Gaeltachta before resigning from RTE altogether to become a barrister and eventually a judge. The next Head of the station was Máire Ní Mhurchú, who had spent a lifetime in the Cork station and we got two new producers of the programme, Aidan Stanley and Dan Collins. I liked their enthusiasm and we got on well together. One afternoon, Máire Ní Mhurchú called me into her office in the last week of a month, when I was in the building, selecting records for that Saturday's programme. I assumed it had something to do with my contract for the next month, but I was wrong. She told me that I wouldn't be required anymore, as Dublin considered my Northern accent was unsuitable for a programme from Cork. This was certainly news to me, after doing the job for a few years. She claimed the decision had been conveyed to her by Michael O'Carroll, her superior from Dublin, who had come down that day.

I wrote Máire a letter straightaway, letting her know that I was resigning immediately, lest my accent would embarrass her or the station any further. I sent a similar letter to Michael O'Carroll in Dublin, apologising for my accent and pointing out that I would not embarrass him any further either, by remaining. I have a tendency not to hang around where I am not wanted – and there were plenty of other things to be doing in those days. Looking through old documents the other day, I came across the letter to Dublin, dated 4 August 1978 and I thought it worth quoting here:

A Mhíchíl, a chara,
    Máire Ní Mhurchú has conveyed to me that yourself and 'Dublin' (!) feel that my Derry accent is not suitable for *Móra Dhíbh* and that my days as a presenter on that programme are numbered. So be it.
    Lest there be any misunderstanding, can I point out that I have had this accent for some time and intend to keep it for some further time, with God's help. I cannot say that I have found it a disadvantage in presenting *Móra Dhíbh* over the last few years.
    In the circumstances, and to save you any further embarrassment on *Móra Dhíbh*, I have decided not to present the two further August programmes (August 12 and 26). To avoid any misunderstanding, I am sending a copy of this letter to the other people involved in *Móra Dhíbh*.
    May I take this opportunity of thanking the *Móra Dhíbh* staff for their kindness and cooperation over the last few years.
    I need hardly say how much I have enjoyed working in radio and look forward to resuming it in different circumstances.
    Beir beannacht,
    Tomás Ó Canainn.

I left a note in the station for the producers and left. They were very surprised and disappointed by the turn of events that had caused me to resign and I think they had sympathy with my case. Some time later, I received a letter from Michael O'Carroll, making no reference whatsoever to the question of my Northern accent, which I had been told was the reason for the non-renewal of my contract. I tried to read from his letter that perhaps he was not the person who had composed that particular story, but that it was someone else, either in Dublin or Cork. My own opinion is that Máire might have gaffed by telling me about my dreadful Northern accent. Whatever else, it was not, especially in those days, politically correct and it was suggested to me by some people inside RTE that I had a case if I wished to push it, but I reckoned it was not worth the effort. Any return to the programme would be missing that first fine careless rapture of the early days, with Pat Twomey from Blarney street on the outside desk at the dawn and Paddy O'Reilly, Eamonn Galvin, Ken O'Callaghan or Mick Fitzgibbon controlling and encouraging from the sound-desk, while Uinsinn, Aidan or Dan checked stop-watches in the background and waved me in for a final round-up before the nine o'clock news pips, timed to come just after our very last note of music – no sooner and certainly no later. A sudden relaxation everywhere then, the challenge of live radio having been met and another small victory won.

IT'S NOT ALL GREEK TO ME

Over the last few years, Greece has assumed an important place in my life. It started with a holiday that Helen and I spent on two Greek islands, Siphnos and Paros, where we moved around looking for accomodation, since we had not pre-booked in Ireland. Greece is a country where finding accomodation in these circumstances is easy and rooms are relatively cheap. Apart from that, not knowing where you'll find a bed for the night, or what it's going to be like, adds to the sense of adventure that is a part of every Greek holiday.

But if I didn't know modern Greece before our first visit, I think I can claim to have had a fair knowledge of ancient Greece, from my schooldays in St Columb's College in Derry. Apart from our five-year study of the ancient language, we read a most interesting book, *Everyday Life in Ancient Greece*, which dealt with the country, its monuments, legends and system of government. Unknown to myself, I probably have had a yen, ever since, somewhere in the back of my mind, to see the country and hear its language. The first time I heard modern Greek spoken was in Cyprus, years ago, when I went there to give a concert with *Na Filí*. I expected that the modern language might not be too difficult for someone who had studied ancient Greek, but I was wrong – so very wrong!

I was introduced to a Greek girl in Cork, Lydia Sapouna, who had come to UCC to do research in Social Work and she agreed to give me tuition in modern Greek. Some time before this a former colleague of mine, Paddy Murphy, had loaned me a record of the songs of Theodorakis, which I liked very much, so Lydia made it a part of our language classes. I had that tape playing in my car on every journey from then on, as I tried to understand what the singers were saying. It was sometimes satisfying, when I listened to songs that Lydia had explained in class, but more often than not,

165

it was a frustrating experience, for the Greeks run their words together in the songs, even more than the Spanish do. We probably do something similar, in our songs, without being aware of it in the way a foreigner might. A knowledge of the Greek alphabet was about the only advantage my study of ancient Greek gave me, but even there, the actual pronunciation of the letters has changed in many cases. Where we used to start the alphabet with the sounds alpha, beta, etc, the modern Greeks say alpha, veeta and they don't actually have a 'b' sounding single letter. To get 'b' they write 'mp', which is a bit confusing at first.

Helen and I really intended going to Cyprus for our first 'Greek' holiday, but changed our mind when Lydia told us about some of the islands and finished up exploring Siphnos and Paros. I learned enough Greek from Lydia in a few months to be able to let the taximan know where we wanted to go in Athens on that first visit. It was Lydia who recommended us to holiday in Siphnos, which is a very beautiful, unsophisticated island, with glorious sunsets, golden beaches and traditional fishing villages. After a week in Siphnos we took a boat, not one of the big ferries that had brought us from Piraeus, but a much smaller craft, to the neighbouring island of Paros. We made friends there with Apostolis, manager of the *Captain Manolis* and spent a very pleasant time in his hotel, named after his father, a retired sea-captain. Apostolis and his cousin Nico ran the establishment and looked for customers at all the incoming ferries, though that is not where we first met them. Those ferries are an important part of the social life of each island, attracting all sorts of islanders, who depend on tourists for a living. We found them a magnet that brought us to the docks every day, just to look at the newcomers and watch the hoteliers' agents inveigling them to whatever hotel they happened to be representing that day. As the *News of the World* used to say in its advertisements for the paper: 'All human life is there.'

The speed and efficiency of the big ferries in turning, landing passengers and taking on a new load was quite astonishing. Not a moment was wasted, with ferry-doors opening while it was still backing up to the quay and starting to close as the last passenger put his foot on board and the vessel swung out into the deep again. But then Greek ferrying was ancient, even in the time of Odysseus!

We took one of the larger ferries back to Piraeus at the end of our holiday and waited for a bus to bring us out to the airport at a very late hour of the night, resisting the taximen who kept telling us that the service was suspended for the night. It was untrue, of course, but an acceptable commercial ploy, I suppose. We didn't fall for it, but waited on with a small group, pretending to be sure of ourselves, as the taximen watched us, like vultures circling their prey! A private car drew up, a girl got out and joined us, and the car, driven by a young man, drove off. Suddenly the girl was in panic: 'I've left my purse with tickets and money in the car. What can I do?'

It transpired that a young Greek fellow had given her a lift from the ferry when she told him that she had to catch a bus from Piraeus to the airport and she had left her purse on the back-seat of his car. We tried to console her and I told her that the Greeks were scrupulously honest, which I believed, and that if the lad found her purse he would get it to her, by hook or by crook. It was a help, I said, that he knew that she was to get a plane back to England from the airport. We had almost given up hope when his car came along at speed and stopped in front of her, with a screech of brakes. Sure enough, it was Sir Galahad returning with the prize. She was overcome with joy and relief, as all of us were, if the truth be told. I told her never to forget that it was in Greece that this had happened – one of the few tourist countries in which such a thing was still possible. Cars are regularly left unlocked there and no one thinks that in any way unusual. Greece, thank God, is not yet Italy, Spain or, dare I say it, Ireland!

When we returned to Cork, I resumed lessons with Lydia, determined to acquire a greater fluency in the language and, I have to admit, pleasantly surprised by my progress to date. The next goal for Helen and myself was Crete, as we knew a number of Irish people who had holidayed there regularly and praised it to the skies. They all agreed with the guide-books that Crete was, in an undefinable way, more Greek than Greece itself. A former colleague of mine in UCC, Paul Brint, put me in touch with a Cretan research associate of his in the University of Hiraklion, who was very helpful and booked us into an hotel in the city for our first night on the island. We found some excellent music in a club that evening and set out next day for Haniá, which had been recommended strongly by Lydia for its Venetian harbour and scenery. Greek buses are a great mode of transport on the islands, as you get a far better view than you would from a car and you don't have the terrifying job of negotiating all those hairpin bends, poised high on the top of sheer cliffs. The trip across the north shore of the island was glorious and Haniá lived up to its reputation for beauty. We found accomodation away from the sea-front, in an old-fashioned house, with very friendly hosts. While we were there, we attended the Easter ceremonies of the Greek Orthodox Church and when we came back to the house on Easter Saturday night, our hosts invited us in to join their partying and feasting, so that we felt that we were part of the community. On Easter Sunday morning lambs were being roasted everywhere on spits that children kept turning, until the lamb was ready for the Sunday dinner. It was a joyous morning in Haniá, with groups of happy Cretans roaming the streets and visiting their friends.

For me, the most exciting thing in Haniá was to come across a small café-bar on the quay, Café Kriti, which had music and dancing every night. The owner, Andreas, was a musician and a top-class dancer to boot! I attended his dancing class almost every evening of our stay there and learned some of the Greek dances well enough to take part in the evening sessions with the locals. We were told originally that the dancing lessons would only be held on Tuesday and Thursday evenings, but when Andreas became aware of how keen I was, he told me to come in at seven o'clock any evening. After that, at about eight o'clock, the other musicians would arrive for their session of playing and singing. They were of a very high standard, most of them semi-professionals who had no gig of their own on that night. Just to sit and listen to them, as you sipped your coffee or drink, was sheer joy. There was nothing commercial about the affair, just genuine Cretan music played and sung by people who loved it. Later in the evening, when a crowd had gathered, the dancing would commence and Andreas would haul me out on the floor to practise my steps with the real dancers.

I went back to Cork after our Cretan holiday determined to give my Greek studies a real push in any way I could. When I heard from Paddy Murphy that one could receive Greek television on satellite, I bought a dish locally and, with Paddy's help, tuned in ET1, the government TV station. Greek newscasters read the news at breakneck speed, so I tended to turn off when they came on, as they did not do me any good at all, psychologically! Regular programmes were much better and I felt I was learning a lot from them. Best of all in many ways were the sub-titled American or British films, as I could hear what was being said in English, while I read the sub-titles in Greek. Apart altogether from its use as a language-learning tool, the ET1 station does a good job, with a high standard of programming, even if they do show far too much of the national Parliament debating chamber for my liking!

We got an unexpected invitation recently to return to the Greek mainland for Lydia's wedding in her home-town of Volos. She was to marry Martin Hodge from Waterford and they had asked me to play pipes at the reception. In Greek Orthodox weddings they don't have music as we understand it at the actual wedding ceremony itself, though there is much chanting by the resident cantor. Surprisingly, the bride and groom do not speak at any time during the ceremony, as all the talking is done by the priest. The cantor, though, promises all kinds of obedience on the part of the bride! I have a feeling that Lydia might have exempted herself from such promises on her behalf. The ceremony was held in a beautiful little church, which was really a cave set into the hillside on the outskirts of Volos. The joined crowns which the priest held over the couple's heads

169

during the ceremony, the little bags of rice which we were all given halfway through, to throw at the happy couple and the individual bags of sugared-almonds we received at the end, all gave the wedding a unique flavour. Some of us went to Lydia's house before going on to the evening reception in the taverna, where we had a feast of innumerable courses and a happy crowd that danced late into the night. We went with Lydia's parents, Alekos and Elli, next day on a tour of the Pilion, the mountain that stretches down the peninsula from the outskirts of Volos. We visited Makrinitsa, an enchanting traditional village set high on the mountain and we dined in a restaurant that gave a magnificent view of Volos and its surrounding plain.

Next day, it was back to Athens to contact Yannis, a Greek friend whom we had met while he was learning English in Cork. We stayed a few days with Yannis in his sister's apartment and went sightseeing to the Acropolis and to Delphi. We had visited the Acropolis on our very first Greek holiday and while it was good to see it again, we were more excited at the prospect of visiting the famous Delphi site, with its temple to Apollo, an ancient stadium, theatre and fine museum. The Oracle at Delphi, with its ambiguous predictions, was something that I had learned about at school, but I hadn't expected such a big area on the mountainside, dotted with little buildings containing the offerings to Apollo from every area in Greece.

Yannis, Helen and myself decided to spend our last full day in Athens shopping. After we had been around the centre for a while, we noticed a TV camera, which seemed to be taking general pictures of the city. Yannis laughingly suggested that we might be on Greek TV that evening. After some more shopping, we came across the camera crew again in a different area, still filming, but we were too busy looking for last-minute gifts to pay too much attention to them. Wandering somewhat aimlessly around Athens was a nicely relaxed way to spend the last day of another Greek holiday, before returning to Cork.

We had been home about a week when Paddy Murphy rang to tell us that his brother in Dublin had just seen us on an English Channel 4 programme about the Greek crisis over the illness of Prime Minister Papandreu. Evidently we were a big part of the television coverage of average Athenians going about their business, notwithstanding the political crisis! A few days later, Lydia returned from Greece to tell us that we had been starring on Greek television as well. She thought it a bit much that she had spent her life in Greece without appearing on television, whereas we had only to spend a week there, attending *her* wedding and could manage a prime-time television spot. Was there no justice?

MUSIC REVIEWING AND COMPOSITION

Someone suggested to me that I should call these memoirs of mine 'Climbing into Dead Men's Shoes', since I had taken over in UCC, from Seán Ó Riada, lecturer in Irish Music, when he died; from Mícheál Ó Riabhaigh, uilleann pipe teacher in the Cork School of Music; and then, in 1980, from Geraldine Neeson, as Music Critic with the *Cork Examiner*.

I knew Geraldine before that time as the wife of Seán Neeson, who had lectured in the Music Department of UCC. I was also aware of her fame as a pianist and piano-teacher. Herself and Seán had been closely involved with radio in Cork, since its earliest days in the Women's Gaol. She had reviewed a number of concerts that *Na Filí* had given in Cork and was very encouraging indeed. She asked me in 1980 to review a few classical concerts that she would not be able to cover. Her daughter Anne subsequently came on the phone to tell me that her mother was very unwell and could I do a number of other concerts that she was contracted to cover. Soon after that, Geraldine died and I was asked by the *Cork Examiner* to continue as music critic. I little thought then that I would still be doing it fifteen years later.

The Irish Times, for whom Geraldine had also worked, asked me to continue as their Cork correspondent. Charles Acton, *The Irish Times* music critic, and Fergus Linehan, the Arts Editor were the two men I was most closely involved with and they were always very helpful. Charles was very careful about how one should present the review to the paper, with a series of rules about whether the word 'opus' should have capitals or not and strict instructions, which I have now forgotten, about K numbers for Mozart and proper Bach numberings. He even had rules about whether the shortened form of the word 'number' should itself be fol-

172

lowed by a full-stop or not. I rather enjoyed making my own rules for such matters in my reviews for the *Cork Examiner*. It was always pleasant to go to Dublin and meet Charles and his wife Carol at a concert or to renew the friendship when they were on one of their infrequent visits to Cork.

On one occasion, when I assume Fergus Linehan was snowed-under with reviews from all over the country, he wrote me a letter, pointing out that my reviews for them were similar to the ones I provided for the *Cork Examiner*. He seemed to be unaware, until I told him, that it had always been that way in Geraldine's time. The subject never came up again and I continued on my merry way, though I think I did try to start and finish the Dublin reports in a different way from the Cork ones. But that small hiccup was not so serious as one that had befallen Geraldine some years earlier, after she had written a review of a string quartet that had played in Cork and sent it in to *The Irish Times*. She was surprised to get a letter back from no less a person than the editor, telling her that this quartet had already been reviewed by Charles Acton in Dublin. Geraldine finally persuaded him that no two concerts were the same, nor were any two reviewers – and her piece was published. A small Cork victory!

Being music critic is a job for which most people have no formal training. Neither did I, though I had some 50 years of listening behind me, a genuine love of the music for its own sake, a B. Mus from UCC and some knowledge of how both professional and amateur musicians approached the problems of public performance. One of my first lessons was learned while I was with *Na Filí*. It concerned the vulnerability of singers. We had been practising for an Italian tour and in one of our pieces I was both singing and playing. Matt said something which implied that my singing was not as good as it might have been. I remember being hurt by his remarks, as, in some way which I did not fully understand, I took the criticism personally, something I would never have done if he had criticised my pipe-playing. Any criticism of my playing would not have bothered me, even slightly – my hands were merely separate mechanical

173

devices that obeyed my instructions about what notes to play, but *my* voice, coming out of *my* mouth, was me. I suddenly understood how vulnerable the singer in public performance is. I think I never forgot that lesson, so that when I did have to say rather negative things about a singer, I tried to do it sensitively.

Of course, one was aware of the strict line that had to be drawn between amateurs and professionals: it was just a matter of wearing the right set of ears for a particular performance! There was always a wide range of performers in Cork, many coming in from abroad for single concerts, though we probably reviewed more amateurs than top professionals.

I was glad to have been reviewing in pianist Charles Lynch's days, though I am told he was past his best when I heard him. I had the pleasure of talking to him about music on a number of occasions and he was always keen to share his wide knowledge. His repertoire, not just of piano-music but of all sorts of music, including opera, was phenomenal. If there was a piano near he would play long operatic redactions to prove a point. I have tried to comment, in a poem, on the difference between his relative slowness of movement and his brilliant keyboard technique:

Charles Lynch

You deceived each time
with your ponderous steps
to the keyboard
we feared
you would not reach:
piano stool protested
as you
slowly
settled heavily
and crouched,
waiting for the last cough
and silence ...

Then, like a child,
you sprang
surprise
of rippling Debussy;

> Chopin shimmered
> from your fingers.

I remember reviewing a soloist who played at one of the lunchtime concerts in UCC. He was the leader of his section in the National Symphony Orchestra and was accompanied by a very good pianist whom he had brought with him from Dublin. I enjoyed the concert and said so, but I made some criticism of a passage in which soloist and accompanist came apart in a fast-moving section. I think I described it in the review as '... with seams showing unashamedly', which I felt gave a graphic impression of what had actually happened.

The soloist wrote to me about it, pointing out that he had asked a number of professional musicians who had been present whether they agreed with what I had said. They told him that they did not. He enclosed a photo-copy of the piece, no doubt intended to put the critic in his place, and asked that I point out to him where this coming-apart had occurred. I was lucky that there was only one such place – a run-up to a climax – in the whole movement, which I marked for him and returned with a letter, telling him not to make critics feel important by taking their comments too seriously, but to continue his good work for music. I did not hear anything else about it and we are still on good terms when we meet.

It is unusual to have a performer write directly to a critic, though it happens sometimes. More likely, they will write to the editor with their complaint. I have, on a few occasions, been given an opportunity by the editor to reply on the same page as the player's letter, something which I have refused to do, since I feel that I have had my chance and he or she should have theirs, if they so wish. When a reply is really necessary, I would rather make it later, so that their view of the matter has had time to make itself felt. Mind you, there are more ways of killing a cat than choking it with butter: I remember a staff-man on a paper phoning to tell me that someone had complained that I had left before the end of a long concert of opera favourites. I think the real problem was that I had made a rather too strong criticism, in my review, of one of the stars. When deadlines are to be met, leaving before the end is quite normal, of course. While performers may thank you for writing a favourable review, I suppose it's only human that they don't thank you for a less favourable one, though logic suggests that they should, since, presumably, each represents your sincere opinion. Their view seems to be that when you write a good review you are undoubtedly right, and even a person of considerable insight, but wrong, as well as deaf, when you pen a bad one!

Musical criticism of professionals is an unusual job. I remember a daughter of mine telling me that she thought it was the most pointless job anyone could possibly have! One of the problems, of course, is that the performer normally knows better than the critic and yet the critic must assess the performance. In a perfect world, s/he would measure it by independent standards that all would recognise and which would not depend on them being able to out-perform the performer. My own position, if I ever had one, was halfway between that and an attempt to be spokesperson for an informed audience, because few people recognise that reviews are read, as often as not, by people who have not been at the concert. If they read you regularly, they like to know what you thought of a particular performance and for some of them, in a perverse way, it establishes a standard they may employ on another occasion.

An important part of the job is simply reasonable communication: nevertheless, particularly in a provincial situation, criticism must have an element of education, if one is truly interested in spreading the good news of music. I am not talking about hype, of course – that is someone else's duty. If your criticism employs too many of the more abstruse words learned on a B. Mus course, you may lose your audience, which may not worry you, though I think it should. One realises, after many years writing about musical performances of all types, that you have an important role as an historian. The paper may not recognise it, but researchers in 100 years from now will, as they try to find out what sort of real music your fellow-citizens listened to in the last century.

The biggest temptation that the critic faces is to show how much he knows. Clearly, it may be useful to put a performance in context by comparing it with others, as long as the matter does not become a mere display. Certain critics feel that by cutting a performance to bits, they show, in some perverse way that I do not understand, that they know more than the performer and much, much more than the members of the audience who were present and thought the playing good. It is worth realising, even though it may be no consolation to the burnt performer, that such a critic's attitude often stems from an inferiority complex about the whole system. In my opinion, the first requirement for a critic is that he or she be honest. Musical ability and knowledge are obviously things one expects, but if honesty is not present, one does not have a critic at all.

It is easy for me to sit back now and look at musical criticism in this way, since I have now resigned from my post as Music Critic with the *Cork Examiner*. For fifteen years I had enjoyed the concerts – some more than others, of course. I was privileged to hear ensembles like the Academica quartet of resident Rumanians, making divine music and their successors, the Vanbrugh, continue that tradition. What else? Mariana Sirbu and Jan Cap playing Beethoven, the Cork Choral Festival, the visits of the National Symphony Orchestra, Barra Ó Tuama's operatic concerts, John O'Flynn's success with the IORC, Geoffrey Spratt's choral work, Bridget Doolan's first lunchtime concert in UCC, Robert Beare's memorable singing *of Is my team ploughing?*, the Jupiter Quintet playing Schubert's *The Trout* and so many more. But important musical moments don't always wait for public concerts. At a party once, I heard a lady singing a love-song for her friends, who included some of her own grandchildren. Her name was Nelly Shannon and her song, for me, stopped the world outside her voice, in a way no one else had ever done. I could hardly wait to get home that evening to tell myself about it in a poem:

NELLY SHANNON, SINGER

Sweep me by the island of your song:
Let swirling slipstream cast me along
That shore, where the trundling world so slowly
Slows and holds its breath. 'You and I,'
It whispers, 'listen; we'll never die.'

I watch, for the very first time,
The miracle of a fragile air and its rhyme
Hold back this sphere's rotating vanes,
Begin to move them in a different sense,
Gently re-ordering our past tense

From a thumbed catalogue of lily-white conventions
Of faithful love, devoid of all the tensions
An airless world winds up around us.
'Shut the book, woman, your song is done:
Listen, the trundling already has begun.'

In a different, but just as effective way, the singing of Áine
Nic Gabhann some years ago in *Messiah*, at the City Hall in
Cork, brought so many feelings crowding into my mind of
past times and partly-forgotten emotions:

PASTORAL

At the City Hall *Messiah*
An alto sang:
He shall feed His flock
Like a shepherd and shall gather
The lambs with His arm
And carry them in His bosom
And gently lead
Those that are with young:
And her song peeled from me
Protective years.

And I was rising for Mass
On a First Friday morning,
Fasting, a bicycle lamp
My dark winter guide
Along the Strand, until
An RUC man quenched
My Catholic light for fear
The Germans might get us
In their sights.

And I was rummaging
In a Paschal bucket

For ashes to bring home,
And I was dipping
My bottle in the holy barrel
Early for Easter water,
And I was garnering
Indulgences for the Holy
Souls in Purgatory
In November, and Father O'Loughlin
With a watery eye was saying
That every tear would be wiped away.

In the 1980s and early 1990s, one always felt there was a welcoming spot in the paper for musical reviews and an ethos which accepted such contributions as a normal part of the overall composition of the page. Music reviews took their place proudly then, in prominent positions on a variety of pages. I have looked in vain for evidence of that ethos over the past year or two. Perhaps some of the blame is mine, for sending in my work directly to the paper's computer by modem from my computer at home. I might have been better advised to keep going in there regularly with my typescript, but I don't think so.

Actual attendance at concerts was not the most difficult part of the job, nor yet the writing of the reviews, though both were time-consuming. The most frustrating side of it all was trying to get a few inches of space in the paper. If there was a space left on the inside back page, that was not covered with death notices or advertisements, one might have a chance, but I often found myself ringing the chief sub-editors every night for a week or a fortnight before a piece would appear. In the meantime, I was being bombarded by questions from artists and their supporters about the non-appearance of the piece. Strange to relate, the music critic was never permitted to have a review on the long-promised musical page, when at last it appeared a few years ago. I never found out what precise qualities one needed to be allowed into that august hyperspace. Lest I give a wrong impression, let me make it clear that I always enjoyed most cordial relations with all of the staff and, I hope, still do.

I wrote to the Editor, to let him know that I was resigning and I tried to make some recommendations about reviewing in general and about music-reviewing in particular. I have to admit that I gave it as my opinion that the paper was not really interested in real reviews, only hype. I waited a fortnight for the reply, which contained just two sentences, one of which said that my letter had been received and its contents noted. That was it, after fifteen years.

Reviewing music is one thing – composing it is quite another! I wouldn't call myself a composer, but I have composed a number of orchestral pieces, a few masses, many choral settings and a handful of pieces for various instrumental combinations. Even though I would like to compose songs, I have hardly touched that side of the art. Looking back on it, I had no doubt at all when I was studying for the B. Mus that I would go on to compose after graduation, and I even had some encouragement in this from Seán Ó Riada, who gave me a book of his, *The Poetics of Music*, written by one of his heroes, Igor Stravinsky, in which the role of music and musical composition is discussed in a series of lectures Stravinsky gave in America. Seán was always helpful and in no way patronising when we discussed my own low-level problems of music-making. But all the spare time I intended to put into composition after those B. Mus days was swallowed up by teaching duties in the Music Department.

Speaking of Seán Ó Riada reminds me of a poem I wrote about him, or rather about those who tried to take him over after his death! One well-known Cork poet expressed strong objection to the very short poem, which is as good a reason as any for repeating it here!

SEÁN Ó RIADA

Jostling poets parse
The silenced nightingale's
Bones, condoning
The stiff-spread wing.

Measure him for a verse,
Now he can no longer sing.

To compose, one has to get inspiration from somewhere. I am not talking about a flash of something in the brain, but about having conditions which make composing easy. The existence of a performer or performers who want new material, whether it is in the shape of a formal commission or not, is a most encouraging starting point. When I was doing the B. Mus, the fact that we had the Cork Symphony Orchestra at our disposal was a great creative spur and I wrote a piece, *Geantraí*, for strings and woodwind for them. I later added some brass and began to feel that I could become a real composer. Things came full circle recently when I wrote a version of it for string orchestra which Hugh Maguire, former conductor of the Irish Youth Orchestra, used at a local music course. We learned a lot about orchestration in our degree studies with Professor Fleischmann, of course, but finding out the practicalities by doing, rather than by talking about it, was a marvellous learning experience.

In our final year of the B. Mus, I decided to do a work for full orchestra which would be a little bit modern, perhaps even daring. I had become very interested in composition based on a tone row, which was, as they might say in Cork, 'da coming t'ing'! Professor Fleischmann approved it in principle, but noted that I hadn't put the name of the work on it. What he didn't know was that I was trying to keep the name hidden until the night of the performance, since it was in bog-Irish with vulgar overtones. My first idea was to call it simply 'Tone Row', but then I decided to put the Irish word for 'my' in front of the title, to give me 'Mo Thone Row' or, 'My Tone Row'. Not satisfied with that, I started my usual game-playing with words, arriving eventually at the name *Póg mo Thone Row*, which sounds a little vulgar, even if it looks all right at first glance. The Professor was inclined to accept it at first, until I hinted at the double meaning. Then he wouldn't hear of such a title going on the programme for the evening concert with the orchestra, even though my student-colleagues and Seán Ó Riada thought it was funny – even clever! Seán asked to see the score and commented favourably on the opening section with its two horns. Conducting the orchestra was a real joy, though my new, rather intellectual composition was lacking somewhat in immediate attractiveness.

Soon after that I was asked by An tAthair Seán Mac Cárthaigh, parish priest of Our Lady Crowned Church in Mayfield, to take over the choir there. The curate was Fr Micheal Ryan, whom I later got to know very well, and there was a welcoming atmosphere in the choir. Some of them are still my friends, years after we have parted musical company. Being involved with a choir made me think of choral composition, so I entered a few works in Oireachtas competitions and won prizes for settings of Irish poems. One of them was a setting for male choir of *Deus Meus*, which Mícheál Ó Súilleabháin conducted at a Choral Society concert in the Aula Maxima and which Fiontán Ó Murchú used often with his very fine choir in St Mary's Dominican Church, Pope's Quay, Cork. Another Oireachtas winner was *Im Aonar Seal*, which I performed with a short-lived Glanmire choir called Cór na Glaise Buí. We travelled to the Oireachtas and, unless I am mistaken, sang another setting of mine, *Rinnce Fada* in the same competition.

The St Mary's Dominican Choir was an inspiration for me, as an amateur composer. In 1978 I was commissioned by the Irish Church Music Association to write a new mass in Irish, *Aifreann Cholmcille*, for their summer school in Dungarvan. Fiontán Ó Murchú was Director of the School that year and he arranged that St Mary's would give the first performance of the mass there, accompanied by my daughters Nuala and Úna along with the *Na Filí* members, Tom, Matt and myself. We had great fun practising each new part of the mass in Cork, as I wrote it and then teaching it later to the participants at the Dungarvan Summer School. I was determined that it would be a happy mass, with a lively entrance antiphon, *Canaigí do Dhia*, which turned out to be a winner. A prayer, common for generations in Connemara and known as *An Phaidir Gheal*, is what I used for a communion hymn. I made the first verse of the prayer a repeating chorus, set to a simple melody: Céard sin ar do láimh chlí? Corp Chríost./Céard sin ar do láimh dheas? Trí braoin d'uisce an Domhnaigh. The prayer was also known centuries ago in England as *The White Paternoster:* 'What is that on your left hand? The body of Christ./What is that on your right hand? Three drops of the water of Sunday'. I remember teaching it to participants at a course once, where another of the tutors was a well-known American liturgical composer. He was bowled over by what he saw as the liberation philosophy of such as: Cár chodail tú aréir? Fé chosa mhic Dé./Cá gcodlóidh tú anocht? Fé chosa na mbocht. 'Where did you sleep last night?/Under the feet of the son of God. /Where will you sleep tonight?/Under the feet of the poor.' He was very taken by the verse which translates as: 'Holy Mary, Mother of God, let me in at the door of plenty, in a place I won't need to ask for food or clothes.' RTE came along and recorded, not only the inaugural mass, but a preliminary rehearsal where people were not afraid to talk and joke. It was only when I heard the recording subsequently on radio that I realised just how happy an occasion the first mass had been.

I was commissioned by the Cork School of Music to write a piece for choir and brass for the School's centenary celebrations and my *Ring Out Your Joy* was performed at their centenary mass in Holy Trinity Church. I always intended to write something else for the same combination, but haven't yet got round to it and probably never will. Talking of what one might or might not do in the future, I am reminded of a saying that used to be common: 'If you want to give God a good laugh, just tell him your future plans!'

I wrote a second mass, a couple of years ago, *Aifreann Naomh Fionnbarra*, commissioned by the organisers of Éigse Uí Ríordáin, which was broadcast on the weekend of the Éigse festival and later used by the College for its UCC 150 Thanksgiving Mass in the Lough Church. I was determined to use a traditional prayer for the communion hymn and was fortunate to be sent a very beautiful one from the Decies district of Waterford: *Íosa Ghil na Comaoineach (Bright Communion Jesus).* Íosa Ghil na Comaoineach, a gheall dúinne buaine do bhia-sa: fuil agus feoil na síoraíochta: tair-se anois fém' dhíonsa: anam agus diacht mo Thiarna. 'Bright Communion Jesus, who promised us your eternal food: the flesh and blood of eternity: come now under my roof: soul and Godhead of my Lord.' I used a poem by Seán Ó Ríordáin, *Cló*, as a recessional. It might not at first sight seem right for the liturgy, but I think it says something spiritually important in what I might call the wider context of our lives: Gach rud dá dtagann, imíonn is ath-thagann is filleann arís ár gcéad ghlóire. 'Everything that comes, goes away and comes back again: our first glory returns.'

I have been asked recently by one of the big Cork choirs to write a four-part mass for them and I am toying with the idea of letting my Greek experience of the Byzantine liturgy influence my musical setting. I know a hymn of theirs to the Blessed Virgin, imploring her aid in time of battle, that would make a wonderful entrance antiphon, particularly if it were scored in the stark Byzantine style. This partly religious, partly nationalistic anthem was sung by the Greeks at critical points in their history, both when they were overrun by the Turks and when they regained their precious freedom. Here's hoping!

Notwithstanding what I said at the beginning about not being a composer, it seems that I may be moving towards the status of liturgical composer, if I continue along the present line. I remember the late Mícheál Ó Ceallacháin, who had written a few masses, saying to me once that if you wrote a mass in Irish, it would always be performed somewhere – nothing more certain. I began to see what he meant recently on a tour of America, when a small group of Irish-Americans came up to me after a concert and sang the *Ár nAthair* from my *Aifreann Cholmcille*. I was moved to find that it meant a lot to them.

My more respectable musical friends might not rate my dance-music as real composition, but I have produced a book of tunes in traditional style, *New Tunes for Old*. Many of these jigs, reels and hornpipes began their life as cranning exercises for my pipe-students and took their name from the student concerned or else from musical friends who liked the particular tune. The late Francey McPeake, on a Cork visit, came into my class and heard me teach a new reel to a young piper. He liked the tune and asked its name – something the tune did not yet possess. I told him that I would call it Theodore Street, in honour of the place in Belfast in which he lived and I still think of Francey when I play the tune. If you are not a traditional music performer, you may not realise that every tune is weighted with memories of places and people – different places, different people – sometimes happy, sometimes sad. Maybe that is what breathes life into music, making it so much more than the sum total of its notes. Stop the ship – I think I have just learned something!

FINALE

The Irish language has plenty of proverbs about things lasting their allotted span and no longer, so if you are an Irish speaker you shouldn't be deceived into thinking things won't change. Yet I continue to be surprised at how big that change has been in my own time. I haven't really been too aware of it as it happened, for change is a thing that only reveals itself in retrospect and no single aspect of my life has avoided it.

When I graduated in Electrical Engineering, there were just three main divisions of the whole field of engineering – Civil, Mechanical and Electrical. I was gradually drawn into the new field of Control Engineering, partly through my research in Liverpool and partly because it seemed to me that the subject had an intellectual and a human dimension not to be found in other branches of engineering. There was, of course, the purely fortuitous circumstance that in my last year in Liverpool University, the lecturer in Control Engineering was due to take up a new post in Australia and Professor Meek had asked me to take-on his Control lectures. Thus, after having gone to Liverpool a Power Engineer, I eventually came to Cork a Control Engineer, full of enthusiasm for this new discipline.

It was interesting to watch the relative decline of Control Engineering as a specialist subject in University courses over the next number of years, possibly due to the emergence of other disciplines associated with microelectronics and power electronics. It seems to me that the basic principles of control have now been assimilated into so many other topics that it is difficult to isolate the elegant theory that always made the subject so attractive for its own sake. Part of the attraction was that control theory could be applied to a range of topics that included anatomy, economics, aspects of human behaviour, robotics, machinery of all types and so on, almost without limit.

I suppose there is no technical field in which there has been greater change than in computing. The progress from building my own analogue computer in Liverpool, through commercial analogue computers we bought off the shelf in the 1960s, to the wonder of punched cards we used in the earliest main-frame digital computers, was a small miracle in itself. I remember the specially designed room in our building in UCC to house a digital computer which couldn't compare, for speed and power, with the tiny lap-top machine on which I am now writing this story! Even the reduction in size of the diskettes used to store information has been phenomenal – it is only a few years since we were handling what we would now regard as monster eight inch disks. How handy the modern small ones that fit snugly into your top pocket!

Every October brings a new generation of students to the University, so you could call this continuous change; but one thing has not changed during my time in UCC – the consistently high intellectual standard of the students coming into Electrical Engineering. One takes it for granted that there will generally be a greater percentage of First Honours graduates in Electrical Engineering than in any other discipline. An unexpected bonus is that the very best students are usually the most humble about their achievements. To put it simply, I have generally found that the best academic students also happened to be among the nicest people in the Department. That is great to remember!

It is wonderful to recall how pleasant it was to be an undergraduate in the Music Department and subsequently a member of staff there. Somehow, one was in closer contact with students there because of our common active involvement with practical music-making. We had many memorable moments. I hope I am not breaking any confessional seals by revealing one of them that comes to mind, when I think of Professor Fleischmann.

We were conducting the practical examination with final year students in the Music Department. As far as I remember, the interviewing Board consisted of Professor

Fleischmann, the external examiner, Professor Denis Arnold, Christopher Stembridge and myself. A female student from Kerry was asked if she thought the overture to the opera *Don Giovanni* was a *pot-pourri* overture, meaning that it contained a number of the themes of the opera, or if it was an independent composition. She gave the question a lot of thought before answering. Her answer showed that she didn't understand the French term *pot-pourri*, but she was determined to get some marks for original thought! 'No,' she said, 'I don't think it has any religious overtones.' It took all my self-control not to burst out laughing. When she left the room, Professor Fleischmann and Professor Arnold tried to fathom what her operatic answer meant, but could not understand, until I explained that she thought they were asking her if it was a 'popery' overture!!

Another examination incident from Electrical Engineering stands out in my memory. The papers on which the students wrote their answers had a space in front entitled *Pas nó Onóracha*? meaning Pass or Honours?' which didn't really apply to Electrical Engineering, as we had no separate pass or honours courses. The grade depended on performance in the examination. A student from an Irish-speaking district in Munster filled the space with his own sardonic comment in bog-Irish: 'Suas chugat-sa', meaning 'up to you!' It didn't compare with incidents that both historian Professor Pender and geographer Professor Charlie O'Connell of UCC used to relate, about getting mass cards from nuns enclosed with their scripts. I think you might call such endeavours 'acts of active faith'.

The two men I have just mentioned were part of the original UCC that I experienced in the 1960s. I don't know how they would have fitted into the later UCC, where money and research grants sometimes clouded the overall aim of the institution. Talking of money reminds me of Jim Hurley, secretary of the College in my early days, who was an avid supporter of the College hurling team and transferred his enthusiasm to many others, including myself. I am sure Jim was largely responsible for my support of the

College team, which met the famous Glen team in County Hurling Finals in those days. A tower of strength and ability in that team was a man who subsequently became President of the College – Michael Mortell. Jim Hurley was famous for watching every penny of the College's money, so that none of it would be squandered. I remember him calling me to task for signing a docket for the Cuallacht, the College Gaelic Society, for which I was Staff Representative. Evidently Jim had less faith in the students' good intentions than I had, and suspected that not all of the money would be used for cultural purposes, even suggesting that the demon drink might be involved. He knew more about students than I did, so he was probably right. Maybe I took a slightly wider view of the meaning of culture!

The city of Cork has changed, of course. Finding a parking space in the centre of town is now an event of real significance, whereas in our first year here, one tended to park outside the first shop and then move off to find a new parking place outside the next one, and so on. Happy days!

On one such Saturday morning, I went into town in my new shining white Cortina and parked it in the middle of the road opposite the Savoy cinema, as I wanted to get a few things in Eason's in Patrick's Street. After that I went to Fitzgerald's on the Grand Parade for a few electrical purchases and spent quite a while there and in the public library. When I returned to Fitzgerald's, my shiny car was gone – stolen! I stopped a police-car and told them my story. They assured me that they would radio my message to other stations and would be on the look-out for my lovely car. I didn't know what to do then, as I was loth to give Helen the bad news about the car, so I went to visit a friend of mine, Brian O'Neill, who lived in Distillery House, on the North Mall. I had been there about an hour talking and drinking coffee, when, in a sudden flash of inspiration, I realised that I hadn't moved my car from its position in the middle of Patrick Street, which meant I had given the Gardaí wrong information. I literally ran the whole way to Patrick Street and saw my shiny white car as I crossed

Patrick's Bridge, patiently waiting for me, just where I had left it. I hopped in and drove it up to O'Neill's, rang the Gardaí to tell them that I had found the lost car and drove home as if nothing had happened. I have often wondered how many times within that hour the squad car had passed the stolen vehicle!

There was a period in the 1970s when horrendous traffic jams were almost normal in the centre of the city. I remember taking the Glanmire bus from the bus-station one evening, only to get completely blocked as we turned from Merchant's Quay on to Patrick's Bridge. After 20 minutes waiting, I decided to abandon the bus and have my tea in the Old Bridge restaurant nearby. I went in, ordered scrambled eggs on toast and had a very pleasant repast. After paying the bill at my leisure, I came out, saw the same Glanmire bus still waiting and boarded again, feeling good. I felt even better when it resumed its journey almost straightaway. The new Cork one-way traffic plan has changed all that, thank God.

We have always felt 'at home' in Cork, not just now, after some 35 years here, but from the very first moment of our arrival. I have no doubt there is a creative something in the air here, but I cannot explain it. I only know that it has been an inspiration to me many times in the past. I have heard other people complain that they are not accepted into Cork society: we have certainly never felt that. It is clearly important, wherever you go, to accept that the natives are the real people of the place and not you. If any change is necessary, then it has to be the visitor who changes, not the long-time resident. Some visitors don't seem to realise this rather obvious fact. Finding out what is important to the people who have lived their lives in a particular place and have helped to establish its traditions is a fascinating exercise.

The Northern 'Troubles' have affected even our position in the South. In the early 1960s, we were accepted by the majority down here as 'our separated brethren' and there was, I think, a general happiness that Northerners were living in the South. But after 1969 things changed a bit. Gardaí were the first to become a little less friendly and a bit more suspicious when they heard the Northern twang. Gone were the days of being told that you had a nice accent. Of course one always has the character who gets the better of a motoring discussion with the unanswerable line: 'Why don't you go back where you came from?' A Northern friend of mine who lived for some time in Carlow was being told the story of a local raid in that town. Her informant confided that the perpetrators 'all had IRA accents'! I thought that was funny, but my friend certainly did not.

Our daughters, Nuala, Úna and Niamh are all involved with music in different ways: Nuala on fiddle, with Macnas in Galway, Úna playing cello with the National Symphony Orchestra in Dublin and Niamh on viola, playing in West End musicals in London. All three of them have played traditional music from time to time, with Nuala currently more involved in it than the others. Music as a career was their own choice, of course, without any parental pushing, though I have to assume that the music they heard all around them through their youth must have had its effect. I often wonder what it must be like to have music as a full-time career. I am not sure that I would like it and, on balance, I am glad it wasn't a real option in my time! I wonder, too, what my childrens' great-grandfather would think of people actually earning their crust by playing music. Times change alright.

I suppose one of the most satisfying changes in my own life has been the transformation from being an English-speaker all the time to becoming an Irish-speaker most of the time. Contrary to what our Advanced Maths tutor in Metrovick in the early 1950s thought, the world-language is English, not Spanish, so I am glad to be a native speaker of English. I have only to broadcast on my amateur-radio transmitter to realise that everyone's back-up language, whether they live in Russia or Timbuctoo is English, making me a very privileged person indeed. But that clearly doesn't conflict with the fact that I am also privileged to have in my mouth the key to the beauties of Irish and its culture, particularly the songs which house so much that is important. They mean more to me than I could possibly explain here. My journey along the learning road of Irish, which has brought me through the gaeltacht areas of Donegal, Connemara, Kerry, Cork, Waterford and Meath has been one of the most satisfying phases of my life, allowing me to meet the likes of seanchaí Micí Sheáin Néill, fiddler Neilidh Boyle, singers Seosamh Ó hÉanaí, Seán 'Ac Dhonncha, Seán de hÓra, Nioclas Tóibín, Darach Ó Cathain and Diarmuid Ó Súilleabháin. All of them have immeasurably enriched my life and I am grateful for that.

If I had been writing a standard autobiography, rather than memoirs, this book would have contained more about my family, but I can't finish without acknowledging how much I have learned about life and love from Helen and my children. They might have been better with a more demonstrative Da and Helen with a more talkative husband, but I hope they have been able to decode my muffled signals of love, affection and of pride in them, down all these years.

We once got Úna a red-setter for Christmas and I stipulated that the place for a dog was not inside, but outside the house. That had always been the tradition in my mother's home in Carnanban, where the dog was a working animal, not really a pet. I always knew, of course, that my harsh rule was only obeyed when I was around, so both sides were happy. When poor Oscar was dying, my daughter Niamh's love for him was heart-breaking. I had the job of burying him in our garden and I learned a lot in doing it. I tried to say what that was, in a poem called *Red Setter:*

> In the tangled roots
> Of ivy and elm
> My spade zings blue sparks
> From stones that begrudge
> You a place in earth,
>
> As I always begrudged you
> The heat of our kitchen,
> Heartlessly ordaining
> That your dozen years
> Should be years of rain.

I cover your head, Oscar
With this heavy stone
Of love, lest an enemy
Burrow to find you
Defenceless at last

And tear the smooth face
That last night drew down
My daughter's kisses
In another lesson
I was too old to learn.

I mute the spade now
That she may not hear me
Putting you with cats
And forgotten hamsters
In this clay of tears.

In writing these memoirs I have come to realise something that I should have known long since – that my mother has been the single biggest influence on my life. Given the fact of my father's death when I was four years of age and my mother's commitment to raising five children, I suppose that was inevitable. Hers was an influence that was always positive and yet never over-powering. In a way we became her life and she surrendered her own life to the job of rearing us. If I went into that in detail, I would become maudlin, so I'll restrict myself to a comment that so many of our friends and relations have made over the years: 'I just don't know how she did it, but she did.' Perhaps a poem I wrote a few years ago when she was buried beside my father Hugh in Drumsurn graveyard might say the last word for me:

TO MY MOTHER

Fifty years of waiting for you and he has become
The clay he entered in January of thirty-five:
I was four then and you were heavy with his fifth child.

This clay the diggers have thrown up is Hugh –
This wet putty-soil of Drumsurn you said
Could not compare with Dungiven's crumbly clay.

That clay was your father Francey, the fiddler,
Biddy Jane, the Stuart he brought to Carnanban,
Your brother Patrick, his daughters Rose and Donna.

But this clay of Drumsurn is my father.

My blurred eyes watch you go where I will not follow;
The rope slips through my palms as we lower you
Bridie, into Drumsurn's dark womb.

Unless all clay be in communion, this is the end
Of our affair, sixty years since we were separated
In Derry, the knot tied and the cord cut.

Your re-marriage the harsh shovels celebrate
And Hugh is patted into place around you with a spade:
I would throw you a rose for your honeymoon, even this late.